INDEPENDENT BAPTISTS...

WHERE WERE WE? WHERE ARE WE?

WHERE ARE WE GOING?

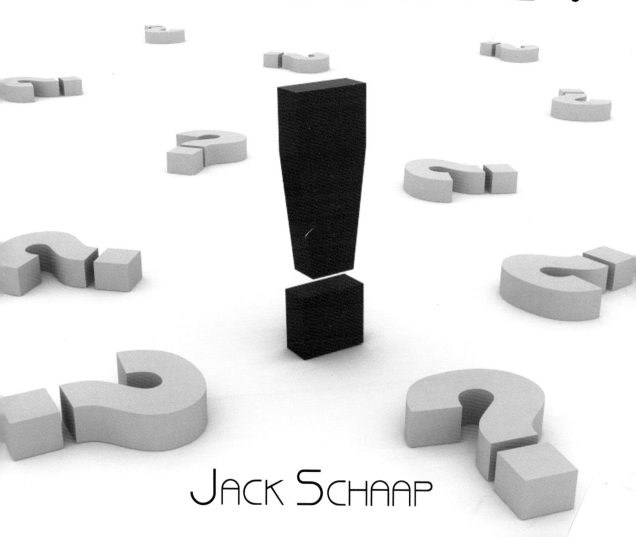

JACK SCHAAP

WHERE ARE WE GOING?

TABLE OF CONTENTS

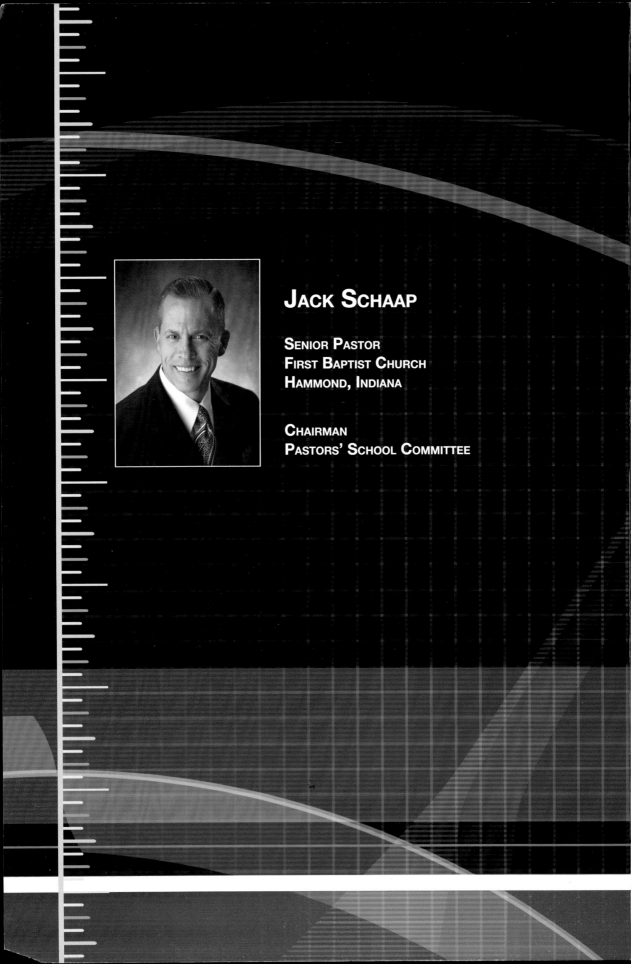

JACK SCHAAP

SENIOR PASTOR
FIRST BAPTIST CHURCH
HAMMOND, INDIANA

CHAIRMAN
PASTORS' SCHOOL COMMITTEE

INTRODUCTION

In 1976 I attended a national *Sword of the Lord* conference in Atlanta, Georgia. I was 18 years old. Thirty-seven nationally known leaders in Fundamentalism were listed in the advertisement for this nationwide conference on soul winning and revival. At that time I added up all the ages of those 37 men, and the average age was 43 years. Some of the men preaching at the conference, such as Dr. Lee Roberson, Dr. John R. Rice, Dr. E. J. Daniels, and Dr. R. G. Lee, were in their 70s and 80s. But if you took away those veteran saints of God, who were born in the late 1800s and the early 1900s, the median age of those preaching was in the 30s.

Those young men, who were the movers and the shakers among soul-winning churches, had established themselves at a young age as being *someone* in Fundamentalism. Truthfully, I was enamored with them, as I was captured by their youthful leadership and their zeal. They seemingly were going to conquer the world for Jesus with their old-fashioned style of Fundamentalism. Their style of leadership was attractive to me, to my generation, and to the multitudes who attended that convention. Thousands of us were held spellbound by their leadership. Men like Dr. Jack Hyles, Dr. Lester Roloff, Dr. Wally Beebe, and Dr. John R. Rice also captured the attention and respect of a generation of us young preacher boys. I, for one, felt I had found "my crowd."

There began a desire in my heart to follow these men, and I was one of many who eagerly sought their signatures in my Bible. I eagerly sought their handshakes and their endorsements on my ministry. I attached myself to them so I could be a part of this body of men who were doing something big for God.

However, less than ten years had passed when that group of 37 had diminished to a small handful—a few by death—others through financial failures, moral failures, marital failures, and other crises which had eroded the leadership that was supposedly steering the ship of Fundamental, soul-winning churches. By the time I reached their average age of 43, which is when I became pastor of First Baptist Church, only 2 of the 37 remained whom I could respect as leaders and mentors, and both of them—Dr. Lee Roberson and Dr. Tom Malone—went to Heaven in 2007. These 37 leaders had left the scene before I turned 50.

At age 50, I stand over the midway point of my preaching career. Thirty-three years ago, I began my ministry among the most aggressive, growing, and influential pastors and churches. I have wondered to myself and have even asked my staff, "Where are the Independent Baptists 33 years later?" And perhaps the most obvious question is, Where are we going?

In 1976 Elmer Towns, dean of the Church Growth Institute at Liberty University, wrote a book about the largest Sunday schools in America. The annual listing of the *"100 Largest Sunday Schools"* was a recognized standard begun by Towns in 1968. His purpose was to show what large churches were successfully doing, which might help other churches do their part in obeying the Great Commission as well. In his book, *The Successful Sunday School and Teachers Guidebook,* he recorded 33 churches, which today would be classified as megachurches (churches which average 2,000 or more per week in attendance). According to Elmer Towns' research, the majority of the largest churches over 30 years ago were Independent Baptist.

Towns' survey concluded that 20 of the 33 megachurches were Independent Baptist churches.[1] From these startling statistics, it seems the Independent Baptists were a profound presence in the church-growth movement and appeared to be making great strides obeying the Great Commission.

The largest of the Independent Baptist churches was pastored by Dr. Jack Hyles, who was recognized as the man behind the world's largest Sunday school.[2] He was described by the *Christian Life* magazine as a pastor who "masterfully injected the old-fashioned Gospel into an expressway society."[3]

When asked, "Why does First Baptist Church of Hammond continue to grow?" Pastor Jack Hyles answered, "Because our growth has been tied to soul winning." The lost are won to Christ in the homes, streets, and factories of the Calumet region of Indiana—busing happens to be the way they get these people to church.[4]

This was the world of Fundamentalism to which I was called.

During the same decade, my predecessor, my former pastor, and my mentor, Dr. Hyles, conducted his own short study of growing Baptist churches across America. His research revealed that the largest church of any kind in 14 states was an Independent Baptist church. It would appear, at least, that Baptists were on their way to doing what Baptists were supposed to do, and that is reaching the lost with the Gospel, getting converts baptized, teaching them to win others to Christ, and reproducing themselves spiritually. They were following God's model, they were preaching God's message, and they were utilizing God's methods.

As you will see in this book, things have changed somewhat in the years that followed. To be honest, I have looked back to what the scenery of church growth was when I entered the ministry and have examined it in comparison and contrast to what I see today, and I have wondered aloud, **"If we Independent Baptists change as much in the next 33 years as we have changed in the past 33 years, will my grandchildren even recognize what their great-grandfather knew as the old-fashioned Baptist way of church building?"**

In this book you will find the research of approximately 30 authors, Bible teachers, pastors, and church-growth authorities. In addition, there were phone callers and data entry personnel which made up an army of nearly 100 volunteers. Many of these are from my own staff, but they have solicited the help of many outside of our ministry. The facts and research are theirs; the final analyses are mine. What you will read is not written to defame or to shame or to discourage anyone. Those who know me personally or professionally know that I am an optimistic realist. My realism compels me to examine the facts and let them speak for themselves. My optimism compels me to examine the facts to see what can be done to correct the mistakes and to further the great work which God has called His churches to accomplish.

Someone has written that the only thing that we learn from history is that we don't learn from history. Well, I commissioned this book because I believe that some of you who read it have the "guts" to tackle the issues and to make the adjustments and to hand to our children and grandchildren healthy, strong, vibrant, and growing churches.

The facts do not present a very pretty picture, but I believe that until we are willing to take an honest look at what we are, we will never make the corrections that are necessary. I want to start by establishing in simple terms what I believe is the model of church growth.

WHAT IS OUR PASSION?

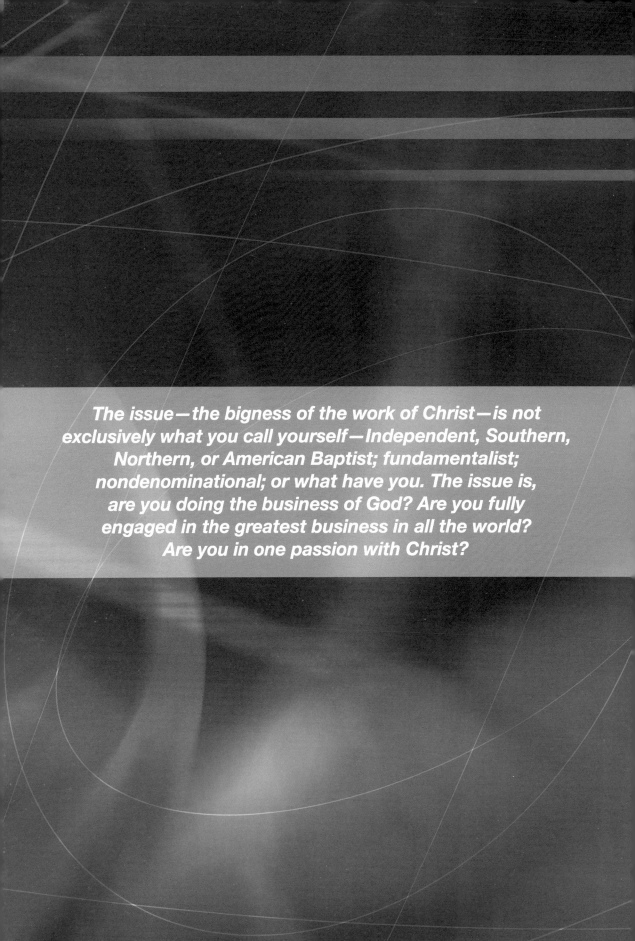

The issue—the bigness of the work of Christ—is not exclusively what you call yourself—Independent, Southern, Northern, or American Baptist; fundamentalist; nondenominational; or what have you. The issue is, are you doing the business of God? Are you fully engaged in the greatest business in all the world? Are you in one passion with Christ?

CHAPTER ONE

THE MODEL

In Luke 2:49 Jesus says, *"...wist ye not that I must be about my Father's business?"* We must ask ourselves, "What did Jesus mean when He said, *'my Father's business'*?" We believe that the Father's business for Jesus consisted of four objectives:

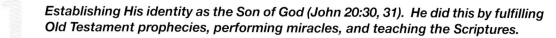

Establishing His identity as the Son of God (John 20:30, 31). He did this by fulfilling Old Testament prophecies, performing miracles, and teaching the Scriptures.

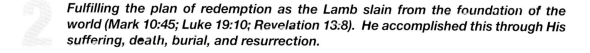

Fulfilling the plan of redemption as the Lamb slain from the foundation of the world (Mark 10:45; Luke 19:10; Revelation 13:8). He accomplished this through His suffering, death, burial, and resurrection.

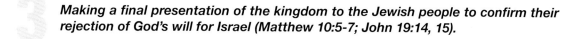

Making a final presentation of the kingdom to the Jewish people to confirm their rejection of God's will for Israel (Matthew 10:5-7; John 19:14, 15).

Founding and commissioning the New Testament institution of the local church (Matthew 16:16–19).

It is this fourth objective of Christ that engages those of us who are in church ministry. I believe the "business" of the local church is what we refer to as the Great Commission. Though the words "Great Commission" are not used in Scripture, the Scriptures record the last words of Christ on earth five separate times. Each of these instances was a record of Jesus' "commissioning" His disciples for the work they were to engage in until He returns to earth. (Matthew 28:19, 20; Mark 16:15-18; Luke 24:47, 48; John 20:21–23; Acts 1:8). This, I believe, is the "business" of the church! And I believe it is the greatest business in all the world. The churches throughout history that have been aggressive about seeing the Great Commission fulfilled both locally and worldwide have, for the most part, been growing churches.

The Great Commission can be stated in four simple words:

GO   DISCIPLE   BAPTIZE   TEACH

The model for church growth was defined by the words of its Founder, and these words are the final admonitions given from His lips moments before He ascended to His Father.

Furthermore, the model is illustrated in Scripture by what I refer to as "the pattern church." God did not leave us without both instruction and example. He instructed us in the Great Commission, and He gave us the example in the church at Antioch of Syria. This is the church where *"...the disciples were called Christians first in Antioch."* (Acts 11:26) This is the church where *"...certain prophets and teachers...ministered unto the Lord...."* (Acts 13:1, 2) This is where these ministers were *"...being sent forth by the Holy Ghost..."* (Acts 13:4) throughout the world.

This church was the headquarters that was responsible for getting out the Gospel to the world. What a pattern ministry! From there the Gospel sounded throughout the whole world. I believe that model is the one churches are supposed to follow today.

As pastor of the First Baptist Church of Hammond, Indiana, I have sought to follow the model of the church started in the book of Acts, particularly the church of Antioch at Syria. I have sought to build a pattern ministry that others could observe and copy. This is what my predecessor, Dr. Jack Hyles, did, and hundreds of churches followed the pattern. Many, if not most, of the growing churches of previous decades got their inspiration as well as their model from this pattern church, which was the evangelistic church of the era.

I am a firm believer in the pattern church philosophy. As our church in Hammond reaches out to foreign nations and establishes strong missions headquarters, we are first building a pattern church in those nations. We want the national pastors, whom we will teach, to observe a pattern church and to copy that church as a model for their nation. We started such a pattern church in Kumasi, West Africa, in October 2006. Fourteen months later, that church averages over 1,000, with a recent high day of 3,416 in attendance. That church has seen over 50,000 converts. It has started a college to train hundreds of men called to preach, with a goal of helping to start thousands of local churches throughout Africa. These young preachers are observing the pattern church and are learning how to model their churches after it. What a powerful force for the "Father's business"! One veteran missionary who recently traveled with me to Kumasi observed the work and stated, "This is how it needs to be done. You have done more in one year in this work than most of us missionaries will see in our lifetime." There is power in a pattern ministry. God knew that when He established that powerful work in Antioch of Syria.

Exploring the Model

In One Accord – One Passion in Reaching the Lost

*The following is an edited excerpt from **Principles of Church Growth** by Jack Schaap.*

One of the primary characteristics of this model that is found in the book of Acts is that the people were all in *"one accord."* The recipe that God used to build the church in Jerusalem from 120 members that were in *"one accord"* in the upper room to several thousand members in two years stems from the concept that *"...they were all with one accord in one place."* (Acts 2:1) Most Christians think that *"one accord"* means that all the Christians got along with each other. However, that is not what the phrase implies. One chapter in the middle of this phenomenal growth tells about Ananias and Sapphira who were killed by God because they lied to the Holy Ghost and stole the tithe and offering promised to the local church.

Also in Acts 6:1 it says, *"And in those days, when the number of the disciples was multiplied, there arose a murmuring of the Grecians against the Hebrews, because their widows were neglected in the daily ministration."* Christians were murmuring and felt neglected. People were upset. Widows were angry with the preachers, and there was a little strife going on. So I can surely infer that *one accord* does not mean that the church members all got along.

> *"The Bible is a pattern Book—a Book of principles given to man from God to guide in making decisions."* – Dr. Jack Schaap
>
> *("Where Do I Stand When the Bible Doesn't Tell Me Where to Stand?" 3/18/07 Unpublished Bible Study Notes)*

If *one accord* means that all Christians must get along with each other to have church growth, then Fundamental Baptist churches have little chance for growth. Many times church members just don't see eye to eye on certain issues. *In one accord* simply means that people are in agreement about certain matters. I am in agreement with my staff men about particular areas of their ministry and responsibilities. We have "one accord" because we agree on that one area.

Literally, *one accord* means "one passion." What is that passion in the book of Acts? Winning souls to Jesus Christ is what it means to be in "one accord." The phrase *one accord* is so vital to understanding why the early church grew from 120 to what some Bible scholars estimate to have been close to 100,000. The church was being persecuted. People were losing their jobs because they were Christians. People were losing money because they were Christians. People were losing friends because they were Christians. That church was growing so fast that the city was scared. The leaders were put in jail and beaten and scolded and threatened, but one thing remained constant—the people were in agreement that the purpose of the local, New Testament church started by Jesus Christ was to get out the Gospel. We call it the Great Commission.[1]

Daily and House to House – Discipling, Teaching, and Mentoring Them

Acts 2:46 says, *"And they, continuing daily with one accord in the temple, and breaking bread from house to house, did eat their meat with gladness and singleness of heart."* To build growing churches requires the discipleship and mentoring of converts. Throughout the book of Acts, references are made to "daily" and "house to house." These terms were not just in reference to getting out the Gospel. It was the fact that the people were sharing doctrine with each other. They continued steadfastly in the apostles' doctrine. Somebody had to teach them. Ephesians 4:8 reminds us that God *"...gave gifts unto men."* For what? *"For the perfecting of the saints, for the work of the ministry, for the edifying of the body of Christ."* (Ephesians 4:12)

The second thing that is consistent in this model is the discipling, teaching, and mentoring of those converts until they reached the point where they replicated themselves in winning others to Christ. II Timothy 2:2 says, *"And the things that thou has heard of me among many witnesses, the same commit thou to faithful men, who shall be able to teach others also."*

The correct model has been in place for centuries—ever since Christ said, *"...upon this rock I will build my church...."* (Matthew 16:18) He established the missions statement of that church through stating the Great Commission, *"Go ye therefore, and teach all nations, baptizing them in the name of the Father, and of the Son, and of the Holy Ghost: Teaching them to observe all things whatsoever I have commanded you...."* (Matthew 28:19, 20) A church that does not follow the correct model may have megagrowth for a single generation, but their failure to prepare themselves for continual growth causes the church eventually to fail.

The model is a passion for souls: evangelizing them, baptizing them, and

> *"It's been interesting to see the models of 'success' change over the years. In the fifties, many of us looked at what Lee Roberson did.*
> *Then the model was Jack Hyles, and then John MacArthur.*
> *Today, Bill Hybels is the model of success for many."*[2]
> – David Wiersbe, son of Warren Wiersbe and pastor of Hope Evangelical Free Church in Roscoe, Illinois

teaching them. Sunday school became that teaching arm of the local New Testament church. Sunday school is school on Sunday for the purpose of *"Teaching them to observe all things whatsoever I have commanded you...."*

The nation's largest churches in the 1970s followed a model predominantly typified by aggressive soul winning, Sunday schools, and the bus ministry. First Baptist Church of Hammond, Indiana, under the leadership of Dr. Jack Hyles, epitomized a model that many Independent, Fundamental Baptist churches were following—aggressive soul winning, "a Sunday school organized on the traditional 10-students-per-class basis, with a small room for each teaching unit,[3] and a bus ministry outreach."

> ***"A church that does not follow the correct model may have megagrowth for a single generation, but their failure to prepare themselves for continual growth causes the church eventually to fail."***

The Independent, Fundamental Baptist church model has been the catalyst for many other denominational churches to grow. One such example is the Phoenix First Assembly of God Church in Phoenix, Arizona, pastored by Tommy Barnett. The church with an average weekly attendance of 15,000 is known as "The Church With a Heart" because of its 240+ outreach ministries.

"I learn from all kinds of people. A Pentecostal kid who goes to a Baptist school picks up a lot. I learned from the late fundamental Baptist Jack Hyles. He had no use for Pentecostals, so I've learned to chew the meat and spit out the bones, so to speak. But he was a tremendous soul winner, and he had great influence in the greater Chicago area. My dad (Tommy Barnett) attended his conference and learned bus ministry from him—bus captains and all of that. We adapted that. Today we have 17 buses that bring inner-city kids to our children's church services on Sunday."[4]

– Matthew Barnett, son of Tommy Barnett and pastor of The Dream Center in Los Angeles, California

Salem Baptist Church in Chicago, Illinois, is another example of a church that sought this Biblical model and the teachings from Pastors' School to help grow their church. The state senator and pastor, James Meeks, who has been the pastor since its beginning in 1985, was very happy to credit Dr. Jack Hyles for helping him to learn four very important things while attending Pastors' School. These four things include:

1. The concept of the Big Day

2. How to soul win

3. How to press a person for a decision during the invitation

4. To receive no negative information prior to preaching

Just recently the Salem Baptist Church was named one of the top-ten fastest-growing churches in the nation.

CHAPTER TWO

THE MESSAGE

One would be hard-pressed to find any pastor of nearly any denomination who would not agree that the Scriptures give us the message we are to preach, that is, if by the message one means the Gospel. Nearly all pastors believe the Gospel is a Biblical message; however, is that exclusively the message we are to preach?

> *"Eventually, our block pastors would share "the Romans Road," the plan of salvation.*
> *We taught them to share four Scriptures and their own testimony.*
> *It's the old Baptist witnessing formula, but it works."*[5]
>
> – Matthew Barnett, The Dream Center in Los Angeles, California

Certainly, I don't fault anyone for preaching only the Gospel. As the Apostle Paul wrote under inspiration in Philippians 1:18, *"What then? notwithstanding, every way, whether in pretence, or in truth, Christ is preached; and I therein do rejoice, yea, and will rejoice."*

One of the difficulties that many of us find in the modern church-growth movement is not that they do not preach the Gospel (the salvation message), it is that they preach almost exclusively the Gospel, unlike the Apostle Paul who preached the whole counsel of God (Acts 20:27).

In a nutshell, I believe the Biblical model for church growth is a Scripturally sensitive model. And I fear that far too many modern models that are being copied by thousands of churches have adopted a culturally sensitive model. Many of these churches believe that God gave us the message, but the model and the methods should be developed more or less exclusively with a cultural sensitivity.

In an article in the May 1997 issue of the Liberty University *Journal*, Dr. Daniel Akin, the Academic Vice President/Dean, School of Theology at the Southern Baptist Theological Seminary in Louisville, Kentucky, made these observations about the Willow Creek model:

> …For many years, a number of us in the Baptist world have wanted to believe in Willow Creek, or at least give it the benefit of the doubt. After all, their church Leadership Conferences are always dominated in attendance by Baptists in general, and Southern Baptists in particular….On careful examination of its ministry, *culture* rather than *Scripture* will be discovered as the force fueling the engine, and it is at this point that church leaders and the flocks that they tend must beware….The church's focus is ill-equipped for producing strong, Biblically grounded disciples.

> Most weekend-seeker services do not include a clear Gospel appeal. This is indefensible. Every time the Gospel is proclaimed in Acts, people were challenged to repent of their sins and exercise faith in Jesus for salvation. Willow Creek should follow in the steps of the first-century church.

> Willow Creek will immerse once a year in the summer and sprinkle twice a year in the winter and summer. Why? Purely pragmatic concerns. The mode of baptism is deemed unimportant and practically problematic, at least when it comes to immersion in December. Scripture is clear that the first-century church baptized only believers and by immersion. However, Willow Creek evidently feels comfortable in jettisoning, or at least complementing, the Biblical model. There appears to be no Biblical conviction at stake, only pragmatic considerations.

> We should pray that the Spirit of God would show the leadership of Willow Creek the errors of their ways in these important areas of ministry and that Biblical truth, rather than cultural compromise, will guide its future.[6]

Independent Baptists have historically taken the position that the Scriptures are the ***FINAL AUTHORITY IN ALL MATTERS OF FAITH AND PRACTICE***. That's a fairly consistent wording for nearly every statement of faith in a Baptist church; however, many Baptists have practically left that position and have used the Scriptures as a final authority only in matters of faith, leaving the "practices" to polls, surveys, experts, seminaries, or cultural trends.

A further problem with leaving the Scriptures for a cultural model in matters of practice is that eventually one's faith, or one's message, becomes diluted by the very cultural impressions and pressures that define one's church-growth model. In other words, once one opens the door for the culture to influence them, that culture begins to influence all areas.

Scripture tells us, *"And be not conformed to this world: but be ye transformed by the renewing of your mind...."* (Romans 12:2) Christianity **IS** a culture of itself! When First Baptist Church started its missions work in Kumasi, West Africa, we stated to the Africans quite bluntly that we were not there to introduce to them an American model, but rather a Biblical model. The Scriptures are not "American." The church is not an "American" institution, and neither is it African. We are not in Africa to conform to African culture. We are there to introduce to the Africans a Biblical model.

This modern cultural sensitivity affects styles of worship, dress, music, and presentation. Albert Barnes states this in his commentary on Romans 12:2:

> ***"And be not conformed..."*** – The word rendered *conformed* properly means "to put on the form, fashion, or appearance of another." It may refer to anything pertaining to the habit, manner, dress, style of living, etc. of others.
>
> ***"...to this world...."*** – τω῀ͺ αίω῀νι τούτωͺ to¯ aio¯ni touto¯. The word which is commonly rendered *world*, when applied to the material universe, is κόσμος kosmos, *cosmos*. The word used here properly denotes an age or generation of people. It may denote a particular generation, or it may be applied to the race. It is sometimes used in each of these senses. Thus, here it may mean that Christians should not conform to the maxims, habits, feelings, etc. of a wicked, luxurious, and idolatrous age, but should be conformed solely to the precepts and laws of the Gospel; or the same principle may be extended to every age, and the direction may be that Christians should not conform to the prevailing habits, style, and manners of the world, the people who know not God. They are to be governed by the laws of the Bible; to fashion their lives after the example of Christ; and to form themselves by principles different from those which prevail in the world. In the application of this rule there is much difficulty. Many may think that they are not conformed to the world, while they can easily perceive that their neighbor is. They indulge in many things which others may think to be conformity to the world and are opposed to many things which others think innocent.[7]

Notice his words *different from those which prevail in the world.* In a recent survey, 80 percent of the largest churches in America admitted they have adopted contemporary Christian music as their preferred method for worship music.[8] Even *TIME* magazine ran an article that stated that teens are being turned off by the worldly music in the modern church growth movement.[9]

They want Bible study and teaching. So much of the "seeker-sensitive" growth model attempts to woo the unsaved into church by "Christianizing" the world's manners.

The Biblical model is for Christians to **"GO INTO"** the world and evangelize each person. Then they are to bring their converts with them to church to be taught the Biblical model of Christianity. The primary purpose of the assembling of the church is NOT to evangelize, but to indoctrinate the church so that the members of the church can go do the evangelizing outside of the assembly.

As the Psalmist despaired in Psalm 79:1, *"O GOD, the heathen are come into thine inheritance...."* What an accurate wording of what is happening today in many growing churches! We are bringing the world's philosophies and culture into the church in an attempt to reach the world. And the result is that the church is failing to represent the Biblical model, and ultimately it will lose its spiritual influence.

I Peter 4:17, 18, *"For the time is come that judgment must begin at the house of God: and if it first begin at us, what shall the end be of them that obey not the gospel of God? And if the righteous scarcely be saved, where shall the ungodly and the sinner appear?"*

Notice that judgment from God will begin at the church (*"house of God,"* I Timothy 3:15). The failure of the local church and thus the judgment from God against the church is that it failed to influence and evangelize those that obey not the Gospel of God. The church's failure to fulfill the Great Commission is the failure to perform God's business.

The church is supposed to change the world, influence the world, evangelize the world—not to conform to the world or embrace the world or use the world to reach the world.

The church is failing to do what Jesus commissioned us to do, and that failure will bring the judgment of God upon us! The nation of Israel was commissioned by God to be His witnesses, but they failed and rejected that commission and were judged by God for conforming to the practices of the heathen countries around them. The church was instituted and commissioned by Christ in response to Israel's rejection, but now many of us are seeing the church reject Christ's commission and begin to adopt the heathen cultural practices of the world we have been called to evangelize and disciple.

The message we preach is not only the Gospel of Christ's death, burial, and resurrection, but also the full counsel of God. The Apostle Paul stated powerfully in Acts 20:27, *"For I have not shunned to declare unto you all the counsel of God."* Again, notice Paul speaking in Galatians 4:19, *"My little children, of whom I travail in birth again until Christ be formed in you."* And again in Ephesians 3:16-19, Paul states, *"That he would grant you, according to the riches of his glory, to be strengthened with might by his Spirit in the inner man; That Christ may dwell in your hearts by faith; that ye, being rooted and grounded in love, May be able to comprehend with all saints what is the breadth, and length, and depth, and height; And to know the love of Christ, which passeth knowledge, that ye might be filled with all the fulness of God."*

And again, notice that declarative section in Ephesians 4:11-15, *"And he gave some, apostles;*

and some, prophets; and some, evangelists; and some, pastors and teachers; For the perfecting of the saints, for the work of the ministry, for the edifying of the body of Christ: Till we all come in the unity of the faith, and of the knowledge of the Son of God, unto a perfect man, unto the measure of the stature of the fulness of Christ: That we henceforth be no more children, tossed to and fro, and carried about with every wind of doctrine, by the sleight of men, and cunning craftiness, whereby they lie in wait to deceive; But speaking the truth in love, may grow up into him in all things, which is the head, even Christ."

It is not sufficient to preach only the Gospel; we must bring them to perfection (maturity) unto the fullness of Christ. And that is one of the powerful omissions in today's Great Commission. The modern church-growth movement has proven they can bring in a crowd, but they are also proving they do not edify the saints and help them *"...grow up into him in all things...."*

Dr. Billy Graham is arguably the most well-known evangelist of the last 60 years. He preached to more than 200 million persons in his Crusades. His message of salvation was clear and unmistakable; millions received Christ as their personal Saviour because of his passion for winning the lost. However, the converts were funneled into every kind of church and nonchurch, Christian and Catholic. These converts were for the most part given only minimal instruction beyond salvation, and though I thrill for everyone who got saved, I grieve that this army of converts was not indoctrinated through Biblical churches. Had these converts been organized to start New Testament churches and to continue in the "apostles' doctrine" daily, just imagine what an impact on the world they would have caused. Millions were saved, but within a generation or two the effects of these millions is negligible on a global setting.

I do not dismiss judgment against myself or any of my soul-winning brethren. Those of us who attempt to win multitudes for Christ and feign ourselves obedient to the Great Commission must examine our message and our teaching and the measure of our effectiveness. I am deeply convicted and provoked by my own failures to indoctrinate the many converts we bring to Christ. ***I believe one of the profound failures of the great soul-winning church-growth movement in Baptist circles is the failure to fully follow all of the Great Commission. We have gone, evangelized, and baptized; but we have failed to teach them "all things."***

CHAPTER THREE

THE METHOD

Growth and blessing come to the degree Christians are willing to disciple and mentor new converts. In Acts 8:4 the Scriptures state, *"Therefore they that were scattered abroad went every where preaching the word."* God brought a great persecution against the church in Jerusalem, *"…And at that time there was a great persecution against the church which was at Jerusalem; and they were all scattered abroad throughout the regions of Judæa and Samaria…."* (Acts 8:1) I believe the church in Jerusalem was growing phenomenally; however, it was not fully obeying the Great Commission of going into all the world. God scattered them by persecution, and they got the message loud and clear. From that point on in the book of Acts, the Gospel went into all the world.

*"For we must all appear before the judgment seat of Christ; that every one may receive the things done in his body, according to that he hath done, whether it be good or bad. Knowing therefore the terror of the Lord, **we persuade men**…."* (II Corinthians 5:10, 11)

So much of the modern church-growth movement is focused on how to get the unchurched into church. But the Biblical method is to get the Christian to **GO** into all the world and to evangelize the world and to bring their converts to the church for baptism and instruction and edifying.

I believe the Biblical method is every-member evangelization. One of the great surges in church growth occurred shortly before I was called into the ministry. That revival of church building was centered around personal soul winning. Men like Dr. John R. Rice, Dr. Jack Hyles, et al. rallied tens of thousands of Christians and motivated thousands of pastors to go soul winning personally. The result was an

> *"The fundamentalist church is the only hope of America. I want to build an influential New Testament church that can be reproduced all over America to help save our nation."*[10]
> –Dr. Jack Hyles

infusion of new converts in the churches and remarkable growth.

In 1974 Elmer Towns recounts in his book, *World's Largest Sunday School: From the Dynamic Ministry of Dr. Jack Hyles*, this illustration about Dr. Hyles' influence on Dr. Curtis Hutson:

> Last year, *Christian Life Magazine* recognized Forrest Hills Baptist Church, Decatur, Georgia, as the fastest growing in the United States, another church influenced by Dr. Jack Hyles. Several years ago, Curtis Hutson read a magazine he was delivering as the part-time pastor and postman. He read in the *Sword of the Lord* that Jack Hyles had baptized 2,000 people in one year. Hutson thought the figure was a mistake—no one could baptize that many—but went to hear Hyles' famous speech on "How to Win Souls." During that sermon, Hutson realized (1) he didn't have a New Testament church, although he preached each week, and (2) it was possible for him to lead

people to Jesus Christ. Two days later Hutson led three people to the Lord, and there has not been a single week in the last five years that he has not won at least a person to Christ. Hutson's church increased from 1,100 to 2,100, qualifying him as the fastest growing church in the nation. This year, Hyles has the fastest growing.[11]

Unfortunately, many of those pastors and churches saw this as a new fad—the latest new method to help them build a church. They did not see this method as a return to the book of Acts and to the original church-building method that God gave us in the Bible. Many of these pastors tried soul winning for a while and then sought out other new methods. The Scriptural method, to put it bluntly, requires a lot of hard work and commitment. It is much easier to bring in a cool, contemporary worship model that will attract the younger generation than it is to put in the "sweat equity" required by obedience to the Biblical method.

A couple of years ago I preached a sermon at First Baptist Church after I had researched those same 14 churches in their corresponding 14 states that Dr. Hyles had researched in 1976. In my research I discovered a disturbing trend that has happened, not just to those 14 churches in those states, but to churches across the country. Only 2 churches in those original 14 still held that title of largest church of any kind, one in the East and First Baptist Church of Hammond, Indiana. I discovered the following facts about the other 12 churches:

Fact # 1   Some churches no longer exist.

Fact # 2   Some are just a fraction of what they once were.

Fact # 3   Some have changed totally and no longer
believe what they adhered to in 1976.

> *"The Scriptural method, to put it bluntly, requires a lot of hard work and commitment."*

My heart was burdened, and in my message were the seeds for this book.

Jesus said, *"…wist ye not that I must be about my Father's business?"* (Luke 2:49) How interesting that the Founder of the church is the only One in the Bible Who refers to His work as business! To put it bluntly, God's business is the greatest business in all the world, and the One Who teaches this is also the One Who said, *"…upon this rock I will build my church…."* (Matthew 16:18) It is so important that we take the work of God as our business on earth.

During my first trip to Ghana, West Africa, in 2006, we traveled to a remote village. After getting off the last road our bus could travel, we hiked on foot to a village where, to our knowledge, the Gospel had never been preached. Over 450 members of that village had waited for over 2½ hours in 95-degree heat to hear me preach. When I finished, over 260 received Christ, and an additional 104 were saved through personal soul winning. A year later a church has been established there, and 370 attend regularly.

What captured my attention most about this village is what happened when the people exchanged gifts with us as a courtesy. We gave them Bibles, and they gave us cases of Coca-Cola. Coca-Cola in a remote village to which we couldn't even drive!? How? A business headquartered in Atlanta, Georgia, saw the bigness of their work—getting Coca-Cola into the hands of every man, woman, and child in the world!

The issue—the bigness of the work of Christ—is not exclusively what you call yourself—Independent, Southern, Northern, or American Baptist; Fundamentalist; nondenominational, or what have you. The issue is, Are you doing the business of God? Are you fully engaged in the greatest business in all the world? **Are you *in one passion* with Christ?**

I met with several of my staff and suggested that we take an honest, hard look at Fundamentalism as it really is. This book is to look at where we were 30-plus years ago, who we are, where we are, why our focus has changed, and attempt to answer the question, Where are we going? In order to assess accurately the premise of this book, we have carefully studied several surveys and have conducted two additional ones. By 2008, of the 1,335 megachurches listed in these surveys, only 27 are now Independent Baptist churches compared to 20 of the megachurches in 1975. We have gone from 61% of the market to 2%! Why?

When the model, the message, and the method are discarded, an identity crisis occurs. Many people who once called themselves Independent Baptists decided that if they shifted the model, that would make the difference. Some of the people who shifted the model the most are now reassessing their position and asking themselves, "Did we do right?" The First Baptist Church of Hammond remains an anomaly. Without changing the model, the message, or the method, the church is still listed in the top 20 of the top "100 Largest U.S. Churches." Why? Well, let's examine some of the facts from the past 33 years.

Where were we in 1976?

In 1890 John Carles Ryle wrote, "There are certain facts in history which the world tries hard to forget and ignore. These facts get in the way of some of the world's favorite theories and are highly inconvenient. The consequence is that the world shuts its eyes to them." His words hold good still but with this difference: the world has long since ceased to care, and the contemporary church dislikes these facts of history. As a consequence, the modern churchman, although not altogether ignoring the facts, interprets them so that he can use them either to support his own ideas or to justify his refusal to tread in the same old paths.[1]

Where Were We in 1976?

"The listing of the nation's largest Sunday schools by *Christian Life* magazine first appeared in 1968, shocking the complacency of the church world."[2] The towns where these churches were located had been captured for the cause of Christ. How? "The reason for the continued expansion of large churches remains the same—dynamic leadership by multitalented pastors who efficiently direct their staff like corporate executives; wear the contractor's hard hat, constructing new buildings; plan advertising campaigns to reach multitudes; yet find time to personally witness to their faith in Christ in their communities."[3] The following information is an examination of the 100 American churches listed by Dr. Elmer Towns as once having the largest Sunday schools.

REASONS FOR SIGNIFICANT GROWTH IN 1976

Most of the churches had vibrant soul-winning and outreach ministries, including the bus ministry.

All of these churches used the Sunday school as the mentoring and teaching arm of the Great Commission.

Some used different mediums of advertising or television exposure.

Many relied on strong preaching and Bible teaching to draw a crowd.

"God blesses unlimited vision, eternal compassion, and continual outreach. As long as these churches possess this spirit, they will continue to remain the largest."[4]

In a nutshell our analysis shows that of the majority of the 100 largest Sunday schools, 73 were Independent Baptist churches. Sixteen of the top twenty churches on that list were Baptist churches. Thirty-three of the 100 largest churches were what would currently be called megachurches, which means the church averaged 2,000 or more. Of those 33 megachurches, 20 proudly claimed the name of Independent Baptist.

"Successful pastors are great scramblers. They can make assets out of liabilities."[5]

– Dr. Truman Dollar

DID THESE CHURCHES REMAIN THE LARGEST?

According to the Hartford Institute for Religion Research in February 2008, out of the 1,335 megachurches, only 27 claim the name of Independent Baptist.[6] In other words the Independent Baptists are no longer the flagships of the nation's largest churches. They have dropped from 61 percent of the market to 2 percent of the market.

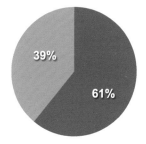

Independent Baptists are no longer the flagships of the nation's largest churches. They have dropped from 61% of the market to 2% of the market.

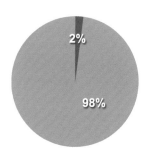

 Independent Baptists   **Other Denominations**

These shocking numbers and statistics all indicate a less-than-favorable analysis of the Independent Baptist movement. Thirty-one years after the 1976 listing was published, another survey was conducted with those 100 churches on Dr. Towns' list. Of the 100 churches surveyed, 67 responded, and the following facts are based upon that 67-percent response rate.

Factoid

74% of churches decreased in attendance since 1976.

59% of the decreasing churches diminished their attendance by more than half.

95% of churches experienced a pastoral change since 1976.

14% of churches DO NOT currently have a traditional Sunday school.

85.2% of churches have gone through a significant building program.

 **78%** of churches have a soul-winning outreach ministry.

3% of these churches actually disbanded, closed their doors, and sold their facilities.

29% of the churches who reported a decline in attendance had stopped soul winning and visitation outreach.

26% of the reporting churches had shown any significant growth. The keys for having significant growth varied, but one observation is that a high percentage of the growing churches added multiple services, including conservative and contemporary services, or multiple service sites, including video.

38% of those who reported having growth in attendance have added soul winning or outreach to their church ministries. These churches previously had no form of outreach.

According to Penn State University, University Park, Pennsylvania, the standard response rate in a five-day calling survey is 36%. (http://www.ssri.psu.edu/survey/Nonresponse1.ppt.)

DECLINING NUMBERS

A quick glance at the survey reveals there was a marked shift in the use of Sunday schools. The common characteristic is that 14 percent of these churches no longer have traditional Sunday schools. In Thom Ranier's book, *High Expectation Churches*, Dr. Ranier conducted a survey of 150 churches in his denomination and 50 from 6 other denominations about the importance of Sunday school. What he discovered troubled and convicted him because he was one of those who had neglected the Sunday school model.

"In almost every church I heard pastors and leaders talk about the role of Sunday school for their evangelistic growth and assimilation. Almost all the leaders said that their sustained growth would have been impossible without the Sunday school. No methodology was deemed more effective than the Sunday school in retaining members."[7]

Dr. Ranier, who serves as the CEO and President of Lifeway Christian Resources in Nashville, Tennessee, and his associates conducted a second more extensive survey of 576 churches in America. He learned once again that the leading churches in this nation value the Sunday school in growing

> *"New Christians who immediately became active in the Sunday school were five times more likely to remain in the church five years later."*[8]

a church. "Nearly 200 of the survey churches indicated that their primary means for members to be involved in the ministry is through the Sunday school. Ministry through the Sunday school is a critical factor."[9]

Thom Ranier conducted his studies predominantly with Southern Baptist churches. He noted that his past research included hundreds of non-Southern Baptist churches. His data indicated that the Sunday school model is the dominant approach for effective assimilation in those churches as well. He concluded,

> *"We have known that Sunday school is a vital component of the past for American churches. Its history is as old as our nation itself. More and more the research indicated that Sunday school is not only our past, it is our future as well. And we who are leaders in the church will ignore this reality to our churches' peril."*[10]

The key characteristic to growth enjoyed by some of the Southern Baptist churches was their return to strengthening their adult Sunday school program. When they discarded the Sunday school model to incorporate more innovative methods, their growth stopped, even decreased. According to a 1997 survey conducted by the Center for Church Growth in Houston, Texas, in 300 sample churches, the top 30 and last 30 churches in 5 categories of attendance were evaluated. The conclusions were as follows:

> *Those churches experiencing growth attributed a larger percentage of their evangelistic growth to the adult Sunday school program.*

Growing churches placed as much emphasis on adult classes as youth classes.

The growing church had smaller adult units of 30 to 60 class members.

Growing churches used challenging Bible curriculum and teaching for adults.

Each growing church organized activities through the adult classes.

Ranier came to the conclusion that the main secret to keeping people in church is to assimilate them into the Sunday school program.

WILL THE REAL AMERICA PLEASE STAND UP?

As already mentioned in the introduction, in 1976 Dr. Jack Hyles conducted research of 14 states in which the largest church of any denomination was an Independent Baptist church. On July 4, 1976, Dr. Hyles preached the sermon "Which One Is America?" at First Baptist Church of Hammond, Indiana. At a Sword Convention the same year, he preached the same sermon and entitled it "Will the Real America Please Stand Up?"

In February 2008 First Baptist Church researchers performed a more in-depth follow-up research on the same 14 churches that Dr. Jack Hyles had researched over 30 years previously. Some alarming truths were uncovered—what has happened to those 14 churches has also happened across the country.

One of these scenarios had taken place in several of the churches:

Disbanded, sold their buildings, and no longer exist.

Downsized greatly and remain just a small fraction of what they once were.

Changed totally and no longer believe similarly to what they believed in 1976.

Only 2 of the 14 still hold the title of the largest church in their state—First Baptist Church of Hammond, Indiana, which is still Independent Baptist, and Thomas Road Baptist Church of Lynchburg, Virginia, which is now a Southern Baptist Church. Where did the other 12 go? The path those 12 churches took indicts today's church-growth movement.

> *"Twenty-five years ago the ten largest churches in Atlanta, Georgia, were Independent Baptist; now, not one of the top ten largest churches in Atlanta are Independent Baptist. Most of them are Southern Baptist."*
>
> – Elmer Towns in a speech at the Southern Baptist Convention to motivate them to have a strong emphasis on souls

The 14 states studied in 1976 by Dr. Jack Hyles and in 2008 by Pastor Jack Schaap were:

1976	February 2008
Florida	
New Testament Baptist Church in Miami – 2,521 (now averaging 2,000)	Calvary Chapel in Fort Lauderdale (Charismatic) – 18,650
Georgia	
Forrest Hills Baptist Church in Decatur – 2,195 (now "very small")	North Point Community Church in Alpharetta (Southern Baptist) – 20,561
North Carolina	
Gospel Light Baptist Church in Walkertown 2,000 (now averaging 2,916)	Friendship Missionary Baptist Church in Charlotte (NBC/ABC) – 6,000
South Carolina	
Florence Baptist Temple in Florence (attendances not available)	Seacost Church in Mt. Pleasant (Association of Relating Churches) – 8,350
Tennessee	
Highland Park Baptist Church in Chattanooga – 9,800 (now averaging <1,000)	Mt. Zion Baptist Church in Whites Creek (Full Gospel Baptist) – 9,000
Virginia	
Thomas Road Baptist Church in Lynchburg – 11,000	Thomas Road Baptist Church in Lynchburg (Southern Baptist) – 15,000
Kentucky	
Beth Haven Baptist Church in Louisville 2,534 (now averaging 250)	Southeast Christian Church in Louisville (Independent Christian) – 17,357

1976	*February 2008*
Michigan	
Temple Baptist Church of Detroit – 10,360 (now disbanded)	Northridge Church of Plymouth (Independent Christian) – 13,865
Ohio	
Akron Baptist Temple of Akron – 6,700 (now averaging 2,500)	The Chapel of Akron (Independent Christian) – 9,570
Pennsylvania	
Bible Baptist Church of Uniontown – (attendances not available)	Sharon Baptist Church of Philadelphia (Southern Baptist) – 5,000
Maine	
Bangor Baptist Church of Bangor – (attendances not available)	Faith Evangelical Free Church in Waterville (Evangelical Free Church) – 720
Indiana	
First Baptist Church of Hammond – 13,561	First Baptist Church of Hammond (Independent Baptist) – 13,000
Illinois	
Bethel Baptist Church in Schaumburg – (attendances not available)	Willow Creek Community Church of South Barrington (Independent Christian) – 23,500
Missouri	
High Street Baptist Church of Springfield – 2,381 (now averaging 1,100)	James River Assembly of God of Ozark (Assembly of God) – 6,717

Of the 14 churches, the mantle of the largest church in the state has been passed to charismatic churches, independent Christian churches, and other denominations. In reviewing the list of the largest non-Catholic churches per state in America from Dr. John Vaughan in February 2008, only one is an Independent Baptist church—First Baptist Church of Hammond.

One southern church averaging well over 2,000 in 1976 and now reporting an attendance of less than 500, utilizes worship teams and holds contemporary services, and according to a staff member since 1976, *"We have tried to change with the times, but our message is still the same. Of course, the bus ministry doesn't work anymore."*

At some time in the past 30+ years, many of the Independent Baptist churches on Elmer Towns' 1975 list of the largest 100 Sunday schools became disoriented, confused, and changed their focus. Some have radically changed their model, their message, and their methods. In essence, they have forgotten who they were, or they never knew who they were.

> *A decade ago 30% of adults claimed to be charismatic or Pentecostal Christians. Today 36% of Americans accept that designation. That corresponds to approximately 80 million adults. One out of every four Protestant churches in the United States (23%) is a charismatic congregation.*[11]

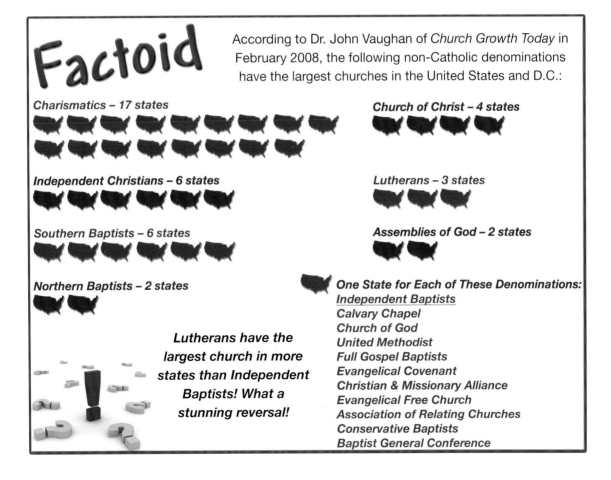

Factoid

According to Dr. John Vaughan of *Church Growth Today* in February 2008, the following non-Catholic denominations have the largest churches in the United States and D.C.:

Charismatics – 17 states

Church of Christ – 4 states

Independent Christians – 6 states

Lutherans – 3 states

Southern Baptists – 6 states

Assemblies of God – 2 states

Northern Baptists – 2 states

One State for Each of These Denominations:
<u>*Independent Baptists*</u>
Calvary Chapel
Church of God
United Methodist
Full Gospel Baptists
Evangelical Covenant
Christian & Missionary Alliance
Evangelical Free Church
Association of Relating Churches
Conservative Baptists
Baptist General Conference

Lutherans have the largest church in more states than Independent Baptists! What a stunning reversal!

The 100 Largest Sunday Schools

from the 1975 *Christian Life* magazine as featured in Dr. Elmer Towns'
book *The Successful Sunday School and Teachers' Guidebook*[12]
Listed on this page are the 33 megachurches, with the Independent Baptist churches highlighted.

Name of Church With City and State	Pastor's Name	1975 Attendance	2008 Attendance	Denomination in 1975
First Baptist Church – Hammond, IN	Dr. Jack Hyles	13,561	13,000	IB
Highland Park Baptist Church – Chattanooga, TN	Dr. Lee Roberson	7,453	<1,000	IB
First Baptist Church – Dallas, TX	Dr. W. A. Criswell	6,703	2,650	SB
Akron Baptist Temple – Akron, OH	Dr. Charles Billington	5,801	2,500	IB
Thomas Road Baptist Church – Lynchburg, VA	Dr. Jerry Falwell	5,566	15,000	IB
Canton Baptist Temple – Canton, OH	Dr. Harold Henniger	4,574	1,400	IB
Landmark Baptist Temple – Cincinnati, OH	Dr. John Rawlings	4,315	1,500	IB
Temple Baptist Church – Detroit, MI	Dr. G. B. Vick	4,043	disbanded	IB
First Baptist Church of Van Nuys – Van Nuys, CA	Dr. Harold Fickett	3,829	disbanded	IB
Trinity Baptist Church – Jacksonville, FL	Dr. Robert Gray	3,776	2,000	IB
Indianapolis Baptist Temple – Indianapolis, IN	Dr. Greg Dixon	3,517	N/A	IB
Calvary Temple – Denver, CO	Dr. Charles Blair	3,418	N/A	ID
The Chapel in University Park – Akron, OH	Dr. David Burnham	3,200	9,570	IB
Madison Church of Christ – Madison, TN	Dr. Ira North	3,185	2,200	CC
First Baptist Church – Hollywood, FL	Dr. Verle S. Ackerman	2,934	<500	IB
First Baptist Church – Jacksonville, FL	Dr. Homer Lindsay	2,846	N/A	SB
First Baptist Church – Riverdale, MD	Dr. Herbert Fitzpatrick	2,308	N/A	IB
Beth Haven Baptist Church – Louisville, KY	Dr. Tom Wallace	2,534	250	IB
New Testament Baptist Church – Miami, FL	Dr. A. C. Janney	2,521	2,000+	IB
Emmanuel Baptist Church – Pontiac, MI	Dr. Tom Malone	2,517	N/A	IB
Bethesda Missionary Temple – Detroit, MI	Dr. James Lee Beall	2,505	1,200	I
High Street Baptist Church – Springfield, MO	Dr. D. A. Cavin	2,381	1,100	IB
Bellevue Baptist Church – Memphis, TN	Dr. Adrian Rogers	2,301	5,100	SB
Northside Baptist Church – Charlotte, NC	Dr. W. Jack Hudson	2,248	1,100	IB
First Baptist Church – Del City, OK	Rev. Bailey Smith	2,235	N/A	SB
First Baptist Church – Lubbock, TX	Dr. Jaroy Weber	2,204	1,600	SB
Forrest Hills Baptist Church – Decatur, GA	Dr. Curtis W. Hutson	2,195	"very small"	IB
Dauphin Way Baptist Church – Mobile, AL	Dr. Jerry Vines	2,185	400	SB
North Phoenix Baptist Church – Phoenix, AR	Rev. Richard A. Jackson	2,159	2,000	SB
Los Gatos Christian Church – Los Gatos, CA	Rev. Marvin G. Rickard	2,089	2,000 (merged)	ND
Gospel Light Baptist Church – Walkertown, NC	Rev. Bobby Roberson	2,058	2,916	IB
Travis Avenue Baptist Church – Fort Worth, TX	Dr. James Coggin	2,047	2,000	SB
Calvary Temple – Springfield, IL	Rev. M. C. Johnson	2,017	N/A	AG

*Current attendances change with regularity as newly reporting churches add information.

The 100 Largest Sunday Schools (continued)

from the 1975 *Christian Life* magazine as featured in Dr. Elmer Towns'
book *The Successful Sunday School and Teachers' Guidebook*
Listed on pages 31–32 are the remaining churches, with the Independent Baptist churches highlighted.

Name of Church With City and State	Pastor's Name	1975 Attendance	Denomination in 1975
Tallowood Baptist Church – Houston, TX	Dr. Lester B. Collins, Jr.	1,989	SB
First Assembly of God – Oklahoma City, OK	Rev. Daniel T. Sheaffer	1,967	AG
Garden Grove Community Church – Garden Grove, CA	Dr. Robert Schuller	1,947	RC
Grace Community Church – Tempe, AR	Rev. Guy Davidson	1,912	ND
Allapattah Baptist Church – Miami, FL	Dr. Donald G. Manuel	1,893	SB
First Baptist Church – Pomona, CA	Dr. Edward Cole	1,882	ABC
Park Cities Baptist Church – Dallas, TX	Dr. Herbert Howard	1,850	SB
Massillon Baptist Church – Massillon, OH	Dr. Bruce D. Cummons	1,842	IB
First Baptist Church – Wichita Falls, TX	Dr. William Pinson	1,840	SB
The Peoples Church – Willowdale, Ontario	Dr. Paul B. Smith	1,839	I
Westside Assembly of God – Davenport, Iowa	Rev. Tommy Barnett	1,825	AG
Dawson Memorial Baptist Church – Birmingham, AL	Dr. Edgar M. Arendall	1,814	SB
Scott Memorial Baptist Church – San Diego, CA	Dr. Tim F. LaHaye	1,801	IB
South Sheridan Baptist Church – Denver, CO	Dr. Ed Nelson	1,777	IB
Good Shepherd Baptist Church – Tampa, FL	Rev. Scotty Drake	1,756	IB
Roswell Street Baptist Church – Marietta, GA	Dr. Nelson Rice	1,726	SB
Moline Gospel Temple – Moline, IL	Dr. Charles Hollis	1,722	FG
Kansas City Baptist Temple – Kansas City, MO	Rev. Truman Dollar	1,703	IB
Bethany First Church of Nazarene – Bethany, OK	Dr. Ponder Gilliland	1,658	N
First Baptist Church – San Antonio, TX	Dr. Jimmy Allen	1,650	SB
Broadway Church of Christ – Lubbock, TX	Dr. Joe Barnett	1,616	CC
Bible Baptist Church – Savannah, GA	Dr. Cecil A. Hodges	1,587	IB
First Baptist Church – Orlando, FL	Dr. Henry Parker	1,587	SB
First Baptist Church – Long Beach, CA	Dr. James A. Borror	1,585	BGC
First Baptist Church – Columbia, SC	Dr. H. Edwin Young	1,578	SB
Bethesda Baptist Church – Brownsburg, IN	Rev. Donald Tyler	1,561	GARBC
Open Door Church – Chambersburg, PA	Rev. Dino Pedrone	1,538	I
Northwest Baptist Church – Miami, FL	Dr. F. William Chapman	1,533	SB
Hyde Park Baptist Church – Austin, TX	Dr. Ralph Smith	1,523	SB
Bethany Bible Church – Phoenix, AR	Dr. John Mitchell	1,508	ND
Calvary Temple – Fort Wayne, IN	Rev. Paul Paino	1,500	I
First Baptist Church – New Castle, DE	Dr. A. V. Henderson	1,498	IB
Reimer Road Baptist Church – Wadsworth, OH	Rev. John Powell	1,488	IB
Cottage Hill Baptist Church – Mobile, AL	Rev. Fred Wolfe	1,485	SB

First Baptist Church – Nashville, TN	Dr. H. Franklin Paschall	1,481	SB
Tucson Baptist Temple – Tucson, AR	Dr. Louis Johnson	1,480	IB
First Baptist Church – Merritt Island, FL	Dr. Jimmy E. Jackson	1,478	SB
First Presbyterian Church – Colorado Springs, CO	Rev. John H. Stevens	1,475	UP
Calvary Baptist Church – Hazel Park, MI	Dr. David D. Allen	1,473	IB
First Church of the Nazarene – Long Beach, CA	Rev. Bill Burch	1,458	CN
Second Ponce DeLeon Baptist – Atlanta, GA	Dr. Russell Dilday, Jr.	1,453	SB
Calvary Baptist Church – Bellflower, CA	Dr. Frank Collins	1,453	IB
Assembly of God Tabernacle – Atlanta, GA	Pastor James G. Mayo	1,448	AOG
First Baptist Church – Midland, TX	Dr. Boyd Hunt	1,446	SB
Canyon Creek Baptist Church – Richardson, TX	Dr. Perry D. Purtle	1,428	IB
Cliff Temple Baptist Church –Dallas, TX	Dr. Richard Ivey	1,416	SB
Broadmoor Baptist Church – Shreveport, LA	Dr. Scott L. Tatum	1,414	SB
Limerick Chapel – Limerick, PA	Rev. Richard Gregory	1,412	I
First Brethren Church – Long Beach, CA	Dr. David L. Hocking	1,405	NFB
Briar Lake Baptist Church – Decatur, GA	Rev. J. Hoffman Harris	1,401	SB
Broadmoor Baptist Church – Jackson, MS	Dr. David R. Grant	1,395	SB
Emmanuel Faith Community Church – Escondido, CA	Dr. Richard S. Strauss	1,385	I
Lima Baptist Temple – Lima, OH	Rev. Ronald Cannon	1,382	IB
First Christian Church – Canton, OH	Dr. E. Richard Crabtree	1,367	CHC
First Baptist Church – Tulsa, OK	Dr. Warren Hultgren	1,367	SB
Greater First Pentecostal – Alexandria, LA	Dr. Gerald Mangun	1,365	UPENT
North Long Beach Brethren – Long Beach, CA	Dr. Geo. O. Peek	1,364	GB
Walnut Street Baptist Church – Lousiville, KY	Dr. Wayne DeHoney	1,363	SB
Tabernacle Baptist Church – Greenville, SC	Dr. Harold B. Sightler	1,360	IB
Abundant Life Memorial Church – Indianapolis, IN	Rev. T. L. Vibbert	1,353	AG
First Baptist Church – Bossier City, LA	Dr. Damon V. Vaughn	1,349	SB
Mt. Carmel Christian Church – Decatur, GA	Dr. Jack H. Ballard	1,347	CHC
Woodland Baptist Church – Winston-Salem, NC	Rev. R. Zeno Groce	1,341	IB
First Baptist Church – Arlington, TX	Dr. Henard E. East	1,339	SB
Ninth and O Baptist Church – Louisville, KY	Rev. LaVerne Butler	1,317	SB
Curtis Baptist Church – Augusta, GA	Dr. Lawrence V. Bradley, Jr.	1,313	SB
Averyville Baptist Church – East Peoria, IL	Rev. Bobby Lounsberrry	1,309	IB

Denomination Abbreviations:

IB	Independent Baptist	ID	Interdenominational
SB	Southern Baptist	GB	Grace Brethren
CC	Church of Christ	FG	Foursquare Gospel
I	Independent	UPENT	United Pentecostal
ND	NonDenominational	CHC	Christian Church
AG	Assemblies of God	AOG	Assembly of God
N	Nazarene	RC	Reformed Church of America
UP	United Presbyterian	GARBC	General Association of Regular
CN	Church of Nazarene		Baptist Churches
NFB	National Fellowship Brethren		
BGC	Baptist General Conference		

Every survey is qualified by how the church reports its attendance, which could be one of three ways:

- Total Membership
- Total Attendance in all Services (including multisite)
- Total Sunday School Attendance

WHO ARE WE?

One of the most respected institutions of our day is the United States Marine Corps, and what sets them apart are their definitions—they know what a Marine is and the heritage of the Marine Corps. The Marine Corps adopted *semper fidelis* as their official motto in 1883. A Latin phrase, *semper fidelis* means "always faithful." What is left unsaid in the motto is also notable. The phrase is "always faithful." It isn't "sometimes faithful." Nor is it "usually faithful," but "always." It is not negotiable. It is not relative, but absolute. Who is always faithful, though, and to what exactly are they faithful? Interestingly, the simplicity of the phrase and the calculated neglect to specify its parameters seems to strengthen it. Marines pride themselves on their straightforward mission and steadfast dedication to accomplish it.[1]

It has long been said that ex-Marines or former Marines do not exist. Once a Marine, always a Marine! Commitment to excellence has built an *esprit de corps* within the ranks of the United States Marine Corps. What sets the Marines apart is their history, their personages, their battles; and every Marine from a cook to a rifleman to a colonel knows and embraces that history. Their heritage makes them "The few, the proud, the Marines." Marines are Marines because of what they believe.

Unfortunately, unlike the United States Marine Corps, what distinguishes Independent, fundamental Baptists is that almost nothing distinguishes Independent, Fundamental Baptists. Many Baptists have lost their heritage.

CHAPTER ONE

WHAT IS A BAPTIST?

The model that the Independent Baptists followed in 1976 was not a model that originated with Dr. J. Frank Norris in the 40s and the 50s, or with Dr. Lee Roberson in the 60s, or with Dr. Jack Hyles in the 70s or 80s, or with any leader in the last 100 years. Baptists have a wonderful heritage of men who were building megachurches before the megachurch movement was ever known as the megachurch movement, and they were Baptist, and they were multiplying their efforts. Keep in mind that Charles Spurgeon pastored a megachurch!

During the Revolutionary War, America was fragilely hanging in the balance, and many historians believe that the Baptist influence not only brought tremendous revival to American soil, but the Baptists also brought about the turning of the war. It is time for Independent Baptists to say, "We have more heritage than just going back to Dr. J. Frank Norris, Dr. Lee Roberson, and Dr. Jack Hyles. Baptist heritage goes all the way back to the Bible." Contrary to popular opinion, the model is not a 1940s or 50s or 60s or 70s or 80s model—it is an ageless model that has been used down through the years since the church at Antioch of Syria. The Biblical, Baptist model has always been characterized by a strong adherence to the Bible.

Many who call themselves Independent Baptists are confused as to what a Baptist is. Today some so-called movers and shakers among Baptists are preaching we are Baptist because John the Baptist was Baptist. John was not part of the New Testament church; he was the last Old Testament prophet. This confusion about our roots leads me to emphasize the fact that *Independent Baptists cannot know where they are going unless they know from whence they came!*

The Trail of Blood by J. M. Carroll is considered the defacto handbook of Baptist history and lineage. Nearly every Baptist historian eventually follows a similar trail to the one that John Milton Carroll established in 1931, which reveals the strong persecution faced by Baptist churches through the centuries from the time of Christ, their Founder, to the present day. The trail of blood left by these Baptist churches shows the endurance and resilience of His model.

Independent, Fundamental Baptists talk about the fact that they are *Independent, Fundamental,* and *Baptist*, but many of them do not know from where those terms came and why they are called *Independent, Fundamental Baptists.* Because so many assume that Baptists began with John the Baptist, they jump forward to J. Frank Norris. Obviously, some Baptist heritage must exist between John the Baptist and J. Frank Norris. Because Independent Baptists do not know what is between, they become easily distracted from their roots.

The book of I Peter was written to stigmatized Christians who had left Judaism. A stigma was *"a distinguishing mark burned in the flesh of a criminal."* I Peter 3:14-16 and 4:1-8 speak of the stigma Christians bear. God says to choose the stigma—the shame and the reproach. To refuse the stigma is to refuse Christ!

How to Escape the Stigma of Christ:

- Drop the name "Baptist."
- Adopt the model of world-pattern services, such as Christian workout rooms and Christian rock 'n' roll.

Baptists get upset because somebody dropped the name of "Baptist" from their church. What upsets me is the Baptists who have kept the name and do not follow the model of Baptist!

– Jack Schaap
"This We Believe…" 1/7/07 Unpublished Bible Study Notes

CHAPTER TWO

DEFINING THE TERMS

An Independent, Fundamental, Separated Baptist

"And he spake unto the children of Israel, saying, When your children shall ask their fathers in time to come, saying, What mean these stones? Then ye shall let your children know...." (Joshua 4:21, 22)

"What Mean These" Words?

When many of us were in Bible college, some fiery preachers knew that if they preached very fervently while saying *Independent, Fundamental, separated Baptist,* they would receive a hearty *amen*. And all who listened to the preachers seemed to know we were supposed to say a hearty *amen* when we heard that phrase.

But when our children ask, "What do these words mean?" we should know that the words *Independent, Fundamental, separated Baptist* are not just buzz words spoken in order to elicit an *amen* from a crowd. These words reflect a wonderful heritage that our children should know.

Each Word Is a Stand-Alone Term.

In the first place, it is important to remember that the words *Independent* and *Fundamental* have entirely different meanings. The term *separated* has a different meaning from the wonderful word *Baptist*.

Though we do not recommend it, it is possible for a person to choose to be an Independent Baptist without choosing to be a separated Baptist. Some have chosen to be Fundamental Baptists, but they have not chosen to be Independent. The term *Independent, Fundamental, separated Baptist* consists of four separate words that convey four separate ideas.

THE TERM *INDEPENDENT*

One of the easiest terms to define is the word *Independent*. An Independent Baptist church is a church that is **not** part of any convention. It is a self-governing, local body; and it is not controlled by any outside group. Independent Baptist churches are not part of the American Baptist Convention, the Southern Baptist Convention, or the General Association of Regular Baptist Churches—they are not associated with **any** convention at all. When you ask Independent Baptist pastors why they are not part of any convention, they most often give three reasons:

1 They believe the Bible teaches that churches are supposed to be local bodies that are not part of a larger denominational structure.

2 They do not believe they should support a convention that uses "even one dime" of their money for unbiblical beliefs.

3 They do not believe they should in any way be forced or encouraged to support missionaries who aren't spreading the pure message of the Bible.

THE TERM *FUNDAMENTAL*

In order to understand the term *Fundamental*, one must understand the blatant heresy that was taught in some German universities during the 1800s. During the 1800s, it was considered prestigious for Americans to travel to Germany for university training. Unfortunately, many German universities taught a theology that was against God and against the Bible. They had the gall to actually teach the topics listed below and others that were equally ridiculous:

- **Moses did not write the first five books of the Bible.**

- **There were at least three "Isaiahs" who wrote and edited the book of Isaiah.**

- **The book of Daniel wasn't a prophecy at all; it was written after the fact.**

- **The Tabernacle of Moses never really existed.**

Fortunately, many Christians reacted strongly against this heresy. Instead of accepting the thoughts of the German theologians, they totally opposed their ungodly ideas. The people who fought against the heresy were called ***Fundamentalists***, and they held to such ideas as those listed below:

- **Moses *did* write the first five books of the Bible.**

- **God inspired the book of Isaiah, and *only one* Isaiah wrote the book.**

- **The book of Daniel *was* a prophecy.**

- **The Tabernacle of Moses *really did* exist.**

Historically, the term *Fundamentalist* means *"a person who **believes** the Bible is the very Word of God, a person who **rejects** the idea that the Bible is merely an ancient document put together without God's inspiration."* Traditionally, Fundamentalists have both strongly believed in the authenticity and authority of God's Word, and they have strongly opposed those who do not believe that. As one historian noted, "Historic Fundamentalism is the literal exposition of all the affirmations and attitudes of the Bible and the militant exposure of all non-Biblical affirmations and attitudes."[2] Another historian made the point this way: "An American Fundamentalist is an evangelical who is militant in opposition to liberal theology in the churches...."[3]

The Fundamentals

In the early 1900s, twelve volumes entitled *The Fundamentals* were published to discredit this modernistic German theology. Few people today know what topics these books contain. Baptists who believe in personal separation might guess that they contain articles about modest clothing or separation from worldliness. But *The Fundamentals* were not written about personal separation; they were written to fight ungodly German theology. Some of the chapter titles include the following:

- *"The Mosaic Authorship of the Pentateuch"* by Dr. George Wright of Oberlin College

- *"One Isaiah"* by Dr. George Robinson of McCormick Theological Seminary in Chicago

- *"The Book of Daniel"* by Dr. Joseph Wilson of Theological Seminary of the Reformed Episcopal Church, Philadelphia

- *"The Tabernacle in the Wilderness: Did It Exist?"* by Dr. David Heagle of Ewing College

The opening of Dr. Wilson's article gives an idea of how the authors clearly combated the German liberals:

> Modern objections to the Book of Daniel were started by German scholars who were prejudiced against the supernatural. Daniel foretells events which have occurred in history. Therefore, argue these scholars, the alleged predictions must have been written after the events. But the supernatural is not impossible, nor is it improbable.

The Fundamentals were written by Bible-believing men, not necessarily Baptist men. A Fundamental professor in an Episcopal seminary wrote the above quotation defending the book of Daniel.

In our day, some Baptists do not believe every word of the Bible was inspired and preserved by God. Though they may call themselves Baptists, they are certainly not *Fundamental* Baptists. A *Fundamental Baptist* is a Baptist who believes the Bible is truly the Word of God, a person who rejects silly notions that the Bible is a famous forgery written by unknown authors and editors.

THE TERM *SEPARATED*

There are two types of separation commonly discussed: (1) ecclesiastical separation and (2) personal separation. [The term *separated Baptist* should not be confused with the Separate Baptists of the eighteenth century.]

Ecclesiastical separation is the idea that a Bible-believing church should not associate with a church that does not believe the Bible. For example, those who believe in ecclesiastical separation believe it would be wrong for the Pope to preach in a Baptist church or for a Baptist pastor to help celebrate mass in a Catholic church.

Personal separation is the belief that God's people should be characterized by holiness (I Peter 1:15, 16; 2:9). Those who believe in personal separation do not all have identical beliefs, but they have beliefs such as these: Christian ladies should wear modest apparel; Christians should avoid indecent, worldly entertainment; Christians should not use vulgar or profane language; etc.

> Separation is not always between good and bad. Separation is built on the doctrine of holiness (Leviticus 11:44). *Holy* means *"set apart by itself; completion or whole."* Uniqueness is lost when the walls of separation are broken down.
> – Jack Schaap
> "This We Believe..." 2/4/07 Unpublished Bible Study Notes

Separation — Why?

Separation is an opportunity for a Christian to express his love in a language God understands. It is an act of love for God by deed.

Separation shows ownership and provides credible evidence that a Christian is a new man and has put on the uniform of Christ.   – Jack Schaap

"This We Believe..." 2/4/07 Unpublished Bible Study Notes

THE TERM *BAPTIST*

The word *Baptist* has more specific meanings than these brief paragraphs can contain, and through the years various acronyms have been developed to present an outline of Baptist distinctives in an easy-to-remember format. The following acronym of Pastor Michael R. Johnson gives a particularly clear idea of Baptist beliefs.[4]

Biblical Authority: II Peter 1:16-21; II Timothy 3:16, 17. In complete contrast to those who believe that the final authority is found in their church tradition or in their personal feelings and experiences, ***Baptists believe the Bible is the final authority in all matters of faith and practice.*** The acid test as to whether a person is a Baptist has always come down to this starting point—Do you believe the Bible is the final authority for all belief and practice? The cardinal truth of the Baptists is, We believe the Word of God is the final authority.

Autonomy of the Church: Matthew 16:18, 19. In complete contrast to those who believe in a complex hierarchy where local congregations receive their orders from higher church powers who may not even live in their nation, Baptists believe in the autonomy of the local church.

Priesthood of all Believers: I Peter 2:9; Revelation 1:5, 6. In complete contrast to those who believe that church members do not have sufficient knowledge or experience to read and interpret the Bible for themselves or to pray directly to the Lord, Baptists believe that Christians can and should pray directly to the Lord and that they can and should read and study the Bible.

Two Ordinances: Baptism (Acts 2:41) and Communion (I Corinthians 11:23-25). Baptists believe very strongly that Biblical baptism is by immersion *after* a person is saved. Therefore, Baptists oppose infant baptism (because an infant is too young to trust Christ as Saviour) and so-called baptism by sprinkling (because it is not immersion). Regarding the Lord's Supper, Baptists believe that the unleavened bread is a reminder of Christ's broken body, and the unfermented grape juice is a reminder of Christ's blood. Baptists do not believe the unbiblical notion that the bread and juice miraculously turn into the actual body and blood of Jesus during Communion.

Individual Soul Liberty: Romans 14:5-12. Baptists believe that each individual is responsible to make personal decisions about what he believes about certain issues. While this idea is balanced with the idea of pastoral authority within the local church, it nonetheless forms a sharp contrast with certain religious groups who believe that church authorities have the power to mandate every detail of a person's life.

Saved, Baptized Membership: Acts 2:47. Baptists believe that no one should be a member of a church unless he is saved and baptized. Further, Baptists believe that the baptism must occur after salvation. This is in sharp contrast to those faiths that believe you can be a member of a church, for example, just because your parents were.

Two Offices: Pastor (Acts 20:28) and Deacons (Acts 6:1-7; I Timothy 3:13). By recognizing only two church offices, Baptists set themselves apart from those who have complex denominational hierarchies. Following the New Testament example of churches that are simple, yet Biblical, in their organization, Baptist churches recognize only the office of pastor and the office of deacon because this is what is set forth in the Scripture.

Separation of State and Church: Matthew 22:21. In these days, some have degraded the term *separation* *of church and state* by saying that it means such things as forbidding the reading of the Bible in the public school. When Baptists use the term *separation of state and church*, they mean that a church should not have a government enforce its wishes. In other words, Baptists believe that people should be able to join a church because they choose to do so, not because the government will punish or persecute them if they do not join the official church of the nation.

Unfortunately, not every Baptist pastor is an Independent, Fundamental, separated Baptist. Each of these terms has a separate, distinct meaning; and clearly explaining the meaning of these terms communicates a wealth of information. Because of our humanity, not everyone who has used these terms has used them with identical scope, some reasoning that the *implications* of a word should be associated with the original term. Despite this variation in usage, there is a core meaning in these definitions that strongly distinguish Independent, Fundamental, separated Baptists from those who deny the authority of God's Word and do not wish to implement its commands in their lives or in the churches they lead. By God's grace, when our children ask, *"What mean these* words?" we will be able to clearly convey this wonderful heritage of our faith.

The foundational truth that supports all that Baptists are is their insistence that **the Bible is the final authority for all faith and practice**—everything that they believe and everything that they follow as a pattern.

That statement is the core essential pillar of all Baptist belief. The motto of First Baptist Church of Hammond is, "We Are People of the Book." Two opposing views to the Independent Baptist view are *progressive interpretation*, which means the Bible needs to be continually reinterpreted as new truth is discovered (which is basically the Catholic and the charismatic philosophy of Bible revelation), and *cultural interpretation*, which is part of the popular modern model stating that because the culture changes, the Scriptures must follow the culture. For instance, many of the most influential models today are considering female pastors, which are patently forbidden in Scripture. It has always been the Baptist position to conform to the Scriptural model—not to conform the Scriptural model to the culture.

CHAPTER THREE

Prominent Spokesmen for Fundamentalism

In this history of ideas, it is common for a powerful truth to have an identifiable point of beginning. After that, prominent leaders trumpet and champion the truth; and as they do this, they often slightly modify and enhance the original idea, sometimes adding slightly different shades to the original meaning. For example, Martin Luther posted his famous *Ninety-five Theses* on the doors of the Castle Church in Wittenberg, Germany, on October 31, 1517. This powerful statement led to the founding of the Lutheran Church; however, it would not be true to say that nothing has happened since 1517 to further define what it means to be a Lutheran. And it would not be true to say that you understand everything there is to know about modern Lutherans if the only thing you know is the *Ninety-five Theses*.

In the same way, Fundamentalism began as a strong reaction against the outrageous and ungodly methods of Bible interpretation that were being taught in some German universities. But as Fundamentalism grew and developed, prominent leaders preached its virtues and denounced its foes; and in the process, they further refined their ideas about what it meant to be a Fundamentalist. In the following paragraphs, we will briefly examine some of the views of Dr. J. Frank Norris, Dr. John R. Rice, Dr. Jack Hyles, and Dr. Curtis Hutson, listed here in order of their birth.

Dr. J. Frank Norris (1877-1952)

Dr. Norris was such a fiery Fundamentalist that some have called him a *"sensationalist"*[5] and described his approach to the ministry as *"violent Fundamentalism."*[6] Of course, the term *violent Fundamentalism*, used here in an academic sense, does not mean at all that Dr. Norris advocated a violent overthrow of the government or anything like that; it simply means that he so powerfully opposed liberals that his approach perhaps seemed violent to those who were part of staid churches that quietly allowed the enemies of the Bible to infiltrate churches.

Perhaps one of the most well-known facts of Dr. Norris' biography is that he amazingly managed to pastor two extremely large churches at the same time, and these two churches were more than 1,000 miles apart. For many years he pastored the First Baptist Church of Fort Worth, Texas, and the Temple Baptist Church of Detroit, Michigan. Dr. Norris' forceful leadership and aggressive church building made it easy for many Fundamentalists to admire him as a great builder, not only as a great believer.

A lesser-known fact is that Dr. Norris' belief in the literal interpretation of the Bible led him to become a believer in premillenialism.

Central to his understanding of the Bible, literally interpreted, and crucial to his preaching was Norris' firm belief in the premillennial coming of Christ. Early and briefly in his ministry he had been a postmillennialist, but Louis Entzminger, his ministerial associate, persuaded him of the error of this position. Thereafter, Norris stressed the premillennialist aspect of the second coming of Christ....[7]

From leaders like J. Frank Norris, Fundamentalists gained passion, aggressive church-building ideals, and a persistent belief in premillennialism.

Dr. John R. Rice (1895-1980)

In describing his own credentials as a Fundamentalist, Dr. Rice is quick to point out that he left the Southern Baptist Convention and became active in Dr. J. Frank Norris'[8] church in Fort Worth.[9] Dr. Rice clearly explained that he believed that a firm belief in the Fundamentals of the faith had definite implications, and he did not believe that a mere passive belief in these doctrines made a person a Fundamentalist in his eyes. Dr. Rice spoke clearly that,

> As we define Fundamentalism, it means a vigorous defense of the faith, active soul winning, great New Testament-type local churches going abroad to win multitudes, having fervent love for all of God's people, and earnestly avoiding compromise in doctrine or yoking up with unbelievers.[10]

While Dr. Rice clearly linked the term *Fundamentalism* to vigorously defending the faith and to aggressive soul winning, he also wrote a chapter entitled "Be a Fundamentalist, But Not a Nut" in which he commented on the King James-only position and describes preaching for Dr. Harry Ironside at the famous Moody Church of Chicago.[11] Dr. Rice wrote a strong chapter entitled "Fundamentalists Should Dress Like Christians," in which he directly states that women's pantsuits are immodest and asserts that women wear *"the stretch kind"* because they want *"to reveal their hips."*[12]

With his emphasis on the *application* of Biblical truth to actively defending the faith, winning souls, living lives characterized by personal separation, and building large soul-winning churches, Dr. Rice extended the term *Fundamentalist* and articulated an idea that led some to use the term *Fundamentalist* to mean approximately what others meant when they said, "Independent, separated, soul-winning Fundamentalist."

Dr. Jack Hyles (1926-2001)

For many years Dr. Rice and Dr. Hyles were compatriots, traveling extensively in meetings together and enjoying a noteworthy personal friendship. Dr. Hyles, ever a believer that Bible doctrine requires Christians **to do** something, had a difficult time describing anyone as a Fundamentalist who did not allow his belief in the basic elements of the Christian faith to lead him to separate from those who did not believe. While some notable Fundamentalists such as W. B. Riley apparently thought the best approach was to remain in a convention and battle for the truth,[13] Dr. Hyles strongly opposed this idea. Though Dr. Hyles did acknowledge that the term *Fundamentalist* was a relative term, he did not approve of using the term *Fundamentalist* to describe someone who did not separate from the liberals and modernists so commonly encountered in conventions.

Note his forceful clarity on these points in his book on *Biblical Separation*.

The term *Fundamentalist* is a relative one, like *conservative* or *liberal*. As it applies to organizations and denominations, *Fundamentalists* would define those who hold to original doctrines and convictions and standards of a movement. This means that at the beginning of a movement all of its adherents would be Fundamentalists. However, movements change….As they do, those who hold to the original doctrines and convictions fight for their preservation and for the return of the movement to its Fundamentals. History tells us that these attempts have failed. Finally realizing that their hopes are futile, a group will pull out of the original movement or denomination and organize another according to the original dogma, standards and convictions of the apostate group. When this happens, the new group can be labeled "Fundamentalists."[14]

> *Quite simply, faith is "what I believe." Practice is "what I do."*
> – Jack Schaap

* * * * *

It is rather popular to define the term *Fundamentalist* as one who believes the Fundamentals; for example, one who believes the verbal inspiration of the Bible….But the term *Fundamentalist* **probably** should not be ascribed to him if he is still a member of an apostate denomination. The name *Fundamentalist* is given not to those who simply believe the aforementioned Fundamentals but to those who have separated themselves from those who do not….**This author**, for example, could not call a member of the American Baptist Convention who believes the verbal inspiration, the deity of Christ, virgin birth, the vicarious death, the bodily resurrection and the second coming of Christ a Fundamentalist….I certainly feel kindly toward [these] men…but in no way could I associate the term *Fundamentalist* with them…until they severed their yoke with the movement which is departing from the faith. If just believing the verbal inspiration of the Bible, the deity of Christ, the virgin birth, the vicarious death, the bodily resurrection, and the second coming of Christ makes one a Fundamentalist, then many who are yoked up with apostate denominations would be classified as Fundamentalists.[15] (Emphasis added.)

Like Dr. Rice, Dr. Hyles extended the term *Fundamentalist*, and he strongly believed that a person deserving of this name was not only duty bound to believe the Fundamentals of the faith but also to separate from those who did not. In this sense, Dr. Hyles would not use the term *Fundamentalist* to describe someone who did not

> *Accountability means "able to give an account of what I believe."*
> –Jack Schaap

practice ecclesiastical separation. For him, the teaching of II Corinthians 6:17 was abundantly clear. *"Wherefore come out from among them, and be ye separate, saith the Lord, and touch not the unclean thing; and I will receive you."*

Dr. Curtis Hutson (1934-1995)

Dr. Hutson certainly believed in the Fundamental approach to Bible interpretation; that is, he would have opposed those who thought the Bible was not divinely inspired or preserved and could be interpreted as the mere words of man instead of as the inspired Word of God. His belief in the literal interpretation of the Bible (the Fundamental approach, as opposed to the liberal approach) allowed him to be confident that the doctrines taught in the Bible are true. In light of all this, he *not only* used the word *Fundamentalist* to indicate a person who believed in the literal interpretation of the Bible, but he used the word to indicate a person who ***actually believed the***

essential doctrines of the Bible, that is, the doctrines of the Bible that are essential to salvation. Note Dr. Hutson's own words:

> Certain doctrines are Fundamental to the Christian faith. I believe everything in the Bible from Genesis to Revelation, but everything mentioned in the Bible is not essential to my salvation. For instance, I could go to Heaven without being baptized.[16]

At the same time, Dr. Hutson did not believe that the term *Fundamentalist* was the correct term to use to describe certain aspects of personal separation. Again, note his own words:

> Another preacher said, *"I am a Fundamentalist. I take vitamin C, vitamin E…and drink carrot juice…."* [This preacher] went on to say, *"I am not only against X-rated movies but all Hollywood movies. I don't believe in playing ball on Sundays. I don't go to the circus, the county fair, or the carnival! I am a Fundamentalist."*
>
> Now that may sound well and good, but it has nothing to do with being a Fundamentalist.[17]

By virtue of who he was, Dr. Hutson reinforced the idea that Fundamentalists should fiercely believe in the Bible, the God of the Bible, and the essential doctrines of the faith; at the same time, his penchant for accuracy apparently led him to prefer the historical use of the term *Fundamentalist*.

Thus, Independent, Fundamental, separated Baptists have a wonderful heritage of Biblical truth and a history of godly men who did their best to bequeath this faith to our generation. It is foolish for us not to know our heritage. In fact, it might even be fatal.

CHAPTER FOUR

Pattern Ministries
of the Last Century

History teaches us that whether our predecessors were the Moravians, Anabaptists, Separate Baptists, Southern Baptists, Baptists have always held to the Biblical model. Because of that stand, model churches have emerged—churches to which others have looked as an example of the application of the model, the message, and the method. Those churches have stood out not only in American history but also in world history.

Baptists have adhered to this model throughout history. They feel a great inflexibility to make any adjustments to the Biblical model of church growth and church building and discipleship. Others have taken great liberty in expanding on that model or making that model applicable to a culture. We believe Christianity is a culture in itself. Because of that, we do not bring the standard up to the men; we bring the men up to the standard, and the standard is established by the Bible. We do not become more worldly to win the lost. We get the lost to a point where they are ready to accept Christ. That is very important because as have learned through history, the church's responsibility is not to stay with the culture or the worldliness of the time. There should be a great difference between where the church is positionally and where the world is positionally so we remain salt in this world and a light in darkness. One cannot remain as light in darkness when he looks like the darkness.

Each one of the following churches has seen strong pastors and strong people who have been dedicated to God's will. Each has accepted the Bible as the final authority. Each church was Biblically separated, and some experienced great difficulty due to the stand they took, only to prevail with God's blessing and help.

The following churches are representative of a pattern in their day and should become a pattern to the preacher who is the student of history. These pattern churches followed the model, preached the message, and employed the methods. Large Baptist churches are not a new phenomenon. Megachurches are not something that was started in the last 30 years. During three-fourths of the twentieth century, Baptist churches owned the market on megachurches. The following examples of large churches (many megachurches) have all copied a very similar model of aggressive soul winning. Of this sampling of churches listed below, some are not very well known, and we wanted to introduce them. We did not include all the churches from Elmer Towns' list, which includes many very well-known churches (see pages 30 – 32).

Highland Park Baptist Church, Chattanooga, Tennessee

In 1942 Dr. Lee Roberson was called to pastor the Highland Park Baptist Church in Chattanooga, Tennessee. Immediately upon accepting the leadership of the church, the emphasis was placed on soul winning and Sunday school. During his ministry more than 61,000 people professed faith in Jesus Christ and followed Him in believer's baptism. In 1947 a new 3,000-seat auditorium was constructed. By 1975 the church averaged over 7,000 in attendance on a weekly basis, and because of their growth a new 6,000-seat auditorium was completed in 1981. In 1946 Dr. Roberson began the Tennessee Temple Schools that have graduated more than 11,500 students, many of whom are serving the Lord in some capacity. You cannot mention the life and legacy of this great man and ministry without telling the story of Camp Joy that also occurred in 1946. This free summer camp, "Where Boy and Girls Begin to Live," was formed because of the sudden passing of his nine-week-old daughter Joy. This camp ministers to about 3,000 young people every summer. The year 1948 brought the beginning of the World Wide Faith Missions program to the church, and the bus ministry was begun in 1949. In 1955 Dr. Roberson led his church to leave the Southern Baptist Convention and begin the Southwide Baptist Fellowship. Dr. Roberson pastored the same church for over 40 years until 1983, when he retired and began to serve as an evangelist.

High Street Fundamental Baptist Church in Springfield, Missouri

Dr. William E. Dowell served as pastor of High Street Fundamental Baptist Church in Springfield, Missouri, from 1941 to 1963. Under his leadership the church grew to an average attendance of 2,700 and telecast its morning services on local stations. In 1950 Dr. Dowell was elected president of the new Baptist Bible Fellowship, and High Street became the first location of Baptist Bible College.

He left Springfield to pastor Jacksonville (Florida) Baptist Temple for five years then returned to serve as executive vice president of Baptist Bible College. In 1974 he became pastor of Baptist Temple while serving at BBC. He retired from the church in 1988 as pastor emeritus. After the death of Dr. G. B. Vick in November 1975, Dr. Dowell became president of Baptist Bible College and served for nine years. From 1984 until his death in 2002, he served as chancellor of BBC, and in his honor the trustees of the school named the field house (largest building on campus) after him.

First Baptist Church of Minneapolis, Minnesota

The First Baptist Church of Minneapolis was pastored by William Bell Riley from 1897–1942. Under his 45-year pastorate, the church reached a membership of 3,000.

First Baptist Church of Dallas, Texas

George Washington Truett pastored the First Baptist Church in Dallas, Texas, for 47 years from 1897 to 1944. He took the church from an attendance of 715 to over 7,000, the largest church in the world at that time. During his pastorate, 19,531 new members were added to the roll.

After the passing of G. W. Truett, Dr. W. A. Criswell became the pastor. Between the years 1897 and 1995, the First Baptist Church had only two pastors. What amazing longevity! Over the years, relocation of the church has often been considered; but as Dr. Criswell once stated, "We are downtown because we choose to be downtown." Dr. Criswell felt that the ministry of the church was more effective in its present downtown location.

First Baptist Church of Fort Worth, Texas, and Temple Baptist Church of Detroit, Michigan

J. Frank Norris, known as the "Texas Tornado" and the "Texas Cyclone," is most often described by biographers as flamboyant and definitely controversial. Norris pastored the First Baptist Church of Fort Worth, Texas. About the same time, he also became the editor of the *Baptist Standard*, a widely circulated Baptist paper that still remains in existence. He was the pastor of First Baptist Church for 44 years. During the 1920s, First Baptist Church was averaging an attendance of 5,200.

In 1935 J. Frank Norris accepted the pastorate of a second church, Temple Baptist Church in Detroit, Michigan. Norris managed to pastor these two churches simultaneously by commuting between Texas and Michigan by train and plane. He continued to pastor the two churches for 16 years. The combined membership of the two churches was over 25,000.

Akron Baptist Temple of Akron, Ohio

In 1934 Dallas Billington held his first church service at the Rimer Elementary School. In one month's time, the church had 81 members. The church officially became the Akron Baptist Temple in 1935. While still holding services in the Rimer Elementary School, the church attendance was skyrocketing; in 1936 the attendance had reached 1,184. By 1939 the attendance averaged between 1,600 and 2,000 every Sunday. The church ultimately grew to a membership of 16,000.

Fundamentalist Baptist Tabernacle/Galilean Baptist Church of Dallas, Texas

John R. Rice saw the need to build an Independent Baptist church in the hotbed of Fundamentalism — Dallas, Texas. The Fundamentalist Baptist Tabernacle was built in 1933. Tragedy struck when the church burned down in 1939. A new church, renamed the Galilean Baptist Church, was built in 1940. The church membership of Galilean Baptist Church was 1,700; more than 8,000 people made professions of faith. John R. Rice left Galilean Baptist Church to go into full-time evangelism and to operate *The Sword of the Lord* paper.

First Baptist Church of Little Rock, Arkansas

Dr. Joe Henry Hankins pastored the First Baptist Church in Little Rock. Under his leadership the church averaged 229 baptisms per year. During a five-year period, the church membership grew to 3,200. Joe Henry Hankins was known to be a great soul winner and a fiery preacher who preached strongly against sin. Dr. Hankins was known for saying, "The reason this world is going to Hell is that not enough people care."

First Baptist Church of Tucson, Arizona

Dr. Richard Beal, the founder of the Conservative Baptist Association, pastored the First Baptist Church in Tucson, Arizona, for 45 years. Starting with a weekly membership of 200 in 1918, the church grew under the pastorate of Dr. Beal to a membership of more than 3,000 members. Twelve other churches were started locally by the outreach ministries of First Baptist Church.

Broadway Baptist Church of Fort Worth, Texas

Broadway Baptist Church was started in 1883 by a 62-year-old preacher named John Gillespie Smith. By the turn of the century, Broadway Baptist had its sixth preacher, John William Gillon, who pastored the church from 1901 to 1905. Under his leadership 500 members were added to the church. In 1906 Broadway called Pastor Price Emmanuel Burroughs, who led the church in adding new buildings and in adding new members to the roll. In 1915 Pastor Forrest Smith accepted the call to Broadway Baptist. During his 15-year pastorate, the church reached a membership of 1,943. The average Sunday morning attendance was over 1,000. From 1930–1935, Broadway Baptist remained a strong church under the leadership of Pastor W. R. White. Pastor Douglas Hudgins became the pastor of Broadway Baptist in 1936. On his very first day as pastor, 1,543 people packed the Broadway Baptist Church. That day 41 new members were added. H. Guy Moore became the pastor in 1947, and the church reached new heights of enrollment numbering 3,450. Although Broadway Baptist Church has had many pastors throughout its history, the leadership ability of the pastors played a key role in keeping Broadway Baptist Church vital. With few exceptions, the people of Broadway Baptist, when faced with calling a new pastor, were wise to choose pastors who had already proven they could grow and pastor a large congregation. Broadway Baptist Church illustrates a people who have remained strong and united in order to see God do something great with their church.

Tabernacle Baptist Church of Raleigh, North Carolina

The Tabernacle Baptist Church started in 1874 when ten members of the First Baptist Church of Raleigh began a Sunday school outreach ministry that became a church. In 1910 the church was running 1,500 in each of its three weekly services. The church has, from its inception, had a heart for missions.

First Baptist Church of Sherman, Texas

The First Baptist Church of Sherman, Texas, was started by R. C. Buckner, who was a true leader of the Baptist movement in the state of Texas. The First Baptist Church took root in Sherman and began to grow. By 1889 the church had 245 members. Revival meetings took place at First Baptist, where men of God like George W. Truett preached. In September of 1914, the church had a membership of 1,357.

First Baptist Church of Jackson, Mississippi

First Baptist was established during the depression years of 1837–1840. W. A. Hewitt became pastor in 1917 and led the church for 28 years. His vision to build an even larger sanctuary was realized in 1926 when the first service in the new building was held. The church grew substantially during the pastorate of W. A. Hewitt. The membership swelled from 800 to 4,500 during his 28-year tenure. Pastor Hewitt was the longest serving pastor of the First Baptist Church. The First Baptist Church has continued to grow and now has a membership of 8,250.

Bellevue Baptist Church of Memphis, Tennessee

During the past 80 years, Bellevue Baptist Church has been led by only four pastors. In 1927 R. G. Lee, who was best known for his sermon, *"Payday, Someday!"* was called to pastor Bellevue Baptist Church in Memphis, Tennessee. R. G. Lee pastored the Bellevue Baptist Church for 33 years until he retired in 1960. The church experienced immense growth under the strong pastoral leadership of Dr. Lee: the membership grew from 1,430 members to 10,000 members.

Calvary Baptist Church of New York City, New York

During the time Calvary Baptist Church was pastored by John Roach Straton from 1918 until 1929, the church experienced great growth. The 2,500-seat church was filled to capacity for nearly every service. Calvary Baptist Church took advantage of technology and was the first church in the country to make regular use of the radio to broadcast its services. In the 1920s, Pastor Straton took a strong stand against evolution. During his ministry, he traveled extensively, encouraging Fundamental Baptists to stay true to the faith. In 1926, Straton led his people to withdraw their church from the liberal Northern Baptist Convention.

First Baptist Church of Philadelphia, Pennsylvania

First Baptist Church of Philadelphia was an impressive, service-oriented church which started with 90 members. Dr. Russell Conwell was its pastor between 1882–1925. Within a decade, First Baptist Church had the largest congregation in America, with a regular attendance of over 3,000. When the church broke ground for a new sanctuary to seat 4,000, it became known as one of the largest churches in the United States.

Walnut Street Baptist Church of Louisville, Kentucky

Walnut Street Baptist Church, founded in 1815 as the First Baptist Church, started with 18 members and met in members' homes. In 1848 the First and Second Baptist churches merged. Their new building had a seating capacity of 600. The congregation stayed in this location until 1902, when the Sunday school attendance went over 1,700. In 1902 the church moved to its present location. After this move the Walnut Street Baptist Church grew to encompass over two city blocks and became known as the largest church in the South. In 1945 the church called Kyle Yates to be the pastor; and under his leadership, the church reached an attendance of 4,000.

As the result of researching these churches, historian Daryl Whitehouse drew several conclusions that these pattern churches as a whole had in common:

- *Strong pastoral leadership is needed for a church to succeed.*

- *Sacrificial living was needed by the pastor and the people of God for the church to succeed.*

- *Support of the pastor by the people was necessary for success.*

- *Service was of the utmost importance (Sunday schools, soul-winning programs, church planting, etc.).*

- *Communication and current technology were used to expand the ministries (radio, television, newspapers, and so forth).*

- *Longevity was the standard for the pastors of these churches. Many of the pastors served their churches for over 40 years.*

- *The pastors took a stand concerning the hot-button issues of the day, such as evolution, modernism, liberalism in the Northern Baptist Convention, etc.*

- *Strength was shown by the pastors and the people in times of adversity.*

- *The pastors had a vision for the church, and the people supported the pastor in his vision.*

- *Growth was the result experienced by all of these churches. These churches did not stray from the model, the message, or the methods.*

CHAPTER FIVE

A HERITAGE OF NOTEWORTHY BAPTISTS

Most modern-day Baptists have no idea who the great Baptists are throughout history. The most quoted Baptist from the past is probably Charles Spurgeon. The Danbury, Connecticut, Baptists to whom Thomas Jefferson wrote, who helped inspire the catalytic phenomenon called the wall of separation between church and state, are still quoted. However, most other Baptists in history are relatively unknown.

Ask any former or current Marine if he recognizes the names Lewis B. "Chesty" Puller, Daniel "Dan" Daly, or John Lejeune, and they will answer with an authoritative "Yes." Ask them if the battles at Chapultepec, Chosin Reservoir, Guadalcanal, Iwo Jima, or Belleau Wood sound familiar, and again they will confidently confirm their knowledge of these historic events. The reason is that these men and these missions are not just remembered; they are revered. The Marines will not let the current men who are serving forget the men who have served.

Ignorance of Baptist heritage causes many Baptists to look at non-Baptists for identity. Because of this, we asked historian and pastor, James Beller, to educate the readers of this book on a brief listing of Baptists. Many men whom we praise for their work in Christianity are those who were not even Baptists. Some of these include, but are not limited to, Billy Sunday, T. Dewitt Talmage, G. Campbell Morgan, D. L. Moody, Sam Jones, and Gypsy Smith. There are also those men we hold high with respect, and yet they murdered and tortured our Baptist forefathers. Four such men include Martin Luther, John Calvin, John Winthrop, and yes, even King James.

In a brief and certainly incomplete research of our Baptist heritage, we found at least 1,200 names of men and women who were recorded for their notable work. These individuals were pioneers of church planting, mission works, authors of music, evangelists, and served in many other areas that helped mold our place as Baptists. Many more have contributed, but this information is simply to confirm and place in the reader's mind that our history does not consist of ten men who were used of God. Many Baptists have long been influential in many areas.

> There is always and forever a pressure push to the left. Christians do not like the pressure, so compromise comes. Fundamentalism has always been "pushed" by music, education, theology, and politics. Each generation must reset that push and periodically push the reset button to stay where they always have been.
>
> – Jack Schaap
> "This We Believe…" 1/14/07 Unpublished Bible Study Notes

The following two lists contain the names of ten Baptists. Five of them are names most will know, and the other five men will probably be unfamiliar to most.

The Baptists that most probably would know would include the following:
1. William Carey – Missionary to India
2. Adoniram Judson – Missionary to Burma
3. David Brainerd – Missionary to the Indians in New Jersey
4. John Bunyan – Bedfordshire, England; author of *Pilgrim's Progress*
5. Roger Williams – Started the first Baptist church in America

Those we probably do not know but should would include the following:
1. Shubal Stearns – church planter who started over 50 Baptist churches from which several thousand churches were started in the South
2. Jeremiah Vardemann – started at least 100 churches of which we know and probably many more; started his last church two days before he died; people would travel several hundred miles to have this well-known evangelist baptize them
3. Samuel Harris – started 60 churches in Virginia while it was against the law to be a Baptist; a convert of Shubal Stearns
4. Daniel Marshall – planted churches in four states; was threatened with incarceration in Georgia as he first declared the Gospel there in 1771[18]; his son Abraham Marshall was widely used of God
5. John Leland – evangelist; close friend of James Madison and helped him fashion the Bill of Rights and the Constitution; preached every Sunday morning in the Capitol and every Sunday afternoon in the Treasury Hall[19]

Another listing of some additional Baptists whose names beg to be studied are: John E. Clough, A.T. Peirson, Christmas Evans, Jacob Knapp, Hezekiah Smith, Samuel Slater, Isaac Backus, Johann Gerhard Oncken, Thomas Hewly, Charles Hughes, James Milton Carroll, John Smyth, John Gill, David Jones, Pastor Weyerburton, Oswald Chambers, Milo P. Jewitt, John Waller, Barnas Sears, and William Rufus Powell.

Adequate credit cannot be given to all the influential men of the Baptist faith who contributed to the success of Baptists in America and the spreading of the Gospel. Baptists have a tremendous heritage and need not look to other denominations for validation, inspiration, or their model of evangelism and church building. The New Testament gives us our model of aggressive evangelism and education, and there is no greater goal for the local New Testament church than to spread the Gospel of salvation and then educate converts to become followers of Jesus Christ.

> *Our forefathers suffered for their efforts to defend the truth. They were maligned, persecuted, and executed so that the true Gospel might continue to be proclaimed, so that people in bondage to error might be delivered into the liberty of Christ.[20]*

CHAPTER SIX

WHY MODELS CHANGE

Having a good understanding of the Biblical model of who we are will help with that identity crisis some Baptists seem to embrace. As I have already stated, straying from the model strongly indicates that Baptists do not know who they are!

Sometime between 1976 and 2008, Independent Baptists began to choose other models, and their first choice was an exciting model called Willow Creek. Interestingly enough, the founder and pastor, Bill Hybels, recently released a book called *Reveal* in which he says, *"Nearly one out of every four people at Willow Creek were stalled in their spiritual growth or dissatisfied with the church—and many of them were considering leaving."*[21] In less than one generation, Willow Creek is now reassessing, reorganizing, rethinking, and restructuring their model because they have said, in essence, "We goofed" in their ultimate purpose. Imagine how these many Independent Baptists who adopted the Willow Creek model must feel when their leader now says, "We need to reorganize the model. We're going in the wrong direction."

The purpose of this book is not to arrogantly pass judgment on those who are different from us, but I think it helpful to hear what leaders from some other models are now saying. *"Numbers can be helpful, but they don't reveal the whole story. Numbers can't peer into the human heart. In an effort to better understand the hearts of people, Willow Creek Community Church undertook a three-year process of study and research to find a way to measure spiritual growth. The results of the study were startling. Long-held assumptions crumbled. And Willow Creek came to grips with the fact that things had to change."*[22]

One of the concerns many of us have with this model is that they are once again surveying the masses to assess their position as a church. Again, as Pastor Hybels did at the inception of his church, the model, true to course, is again following a cultural sensitivity. Pastor Hybels is, by his own admission, a personal soul winner, and he has written a bestseller on this topic; however, the Willow Creek model, as with many other contemporary churches, strays from a Scriptural sensitivity as to church growth and edification and establishes the basis for its philosophy of church growth on a cultural sensitivity.

Certainly, other models exist which have been successful as far as numerical numbers. Some churches on Elmer Towns' 1976 survey of the top 100 churches were not Independent Baptists. Tommy Barnett, who was mentioned in the first section, is not an Independent Fundamental Baptist, but he has found a model that works. And he has not changed his model. Tommy Barnett credits past growth and continual growth of their church to their adopting key elements of the Independent Baptist model.

Much confusion comes from rethinking which model to follow. With these thoughts in mind, let's examine why models change.

1.   *Change comes because of cultural pressure.*

Cultural change creates an enormous pressure to change the music, change the standards, change the dress, and change the approach to growth. However, the model shouldn't change because of persecution and pressure. God's way of blessing is often the path of suffering.

> Persecution has been a part of the lives of Christians for centuries. Obviously, a Satanic attack has been waged upon Christianity since its beginning, but humanly speaking, every man wants to believe that his religion is **the** religion. Consequently, when Scripture was fulfilled and Christianity came into existence, Christianity began to grow and other religions began to fear the newfound religion. They began to attack the leaders and the followers. In spite of being attacked, Christianity still grew. [23]

2.   *Change comes because of misunderstanding the model.*

A preacher may proudly proclaim, *"I am an Independent, Fundamental, separated, soul-winning Baptist,"* and have no idea what that nomenclature means. If he doesn't succeed at building a church, he blames the model and says, *"Independent, Fundamental, separated, soul-winning Baptists are wrong."* Some who are reconsidering their position need to know from where they came and where they are before they begin to make fairly immature jumps from model to model.

3.   *Change comes because of a disoriented perspective.*

Some leaders believe that in order to grow they must "divorce" themselves from terms such as *Fundamentalism.* Their model has become the community church model. Those who choose this model also drop the name of "Baptist"— basically because they do not know what it means to be a Baptist. They somehow think that titles and names interfere with the message. Perhaps they should also consider not talking about the CROSS, which is highly offensive, or perhaps they should poll their community to find what definition of Christianity and the Gospel is best suited for the cultural tastes and traditions of the neighborhood. How different this is from the strong, plain teaching of Christ!

4.   *Change comes when the founding pastor goes off the scene, and the next man is separated from the roots of the Biblical model.*

The young man coming on the scene looks for a new way to identify his own leadership to set himself apart, so he chooses a new model. I believe the Holy Ghost addresses this through Paul in I Timothy 3:6, *"Not a novice, lest being lifted up with pride he fall into the condemnation of the devil."* The immaturity of some of the pastors assuming the pulpits from their predecessors explains this insecure need to track a new course. This is nothing more than pride; and it is, at best, self-motivated if not Satanically inspired, as Paul wrote.

CHAPTER SEVEN

CAN OTHER MODELS BE SUCCESSFUL?

Allow me to address a particularly sensitive issue among those who believe they have the Biblically correct church-growth model. Is it possible that some of these large, growing churches which have adopted contemporary models of church growth are being blessed by God and that their modern model is actually successful? Yes, it is possible. While I believe there is a definite Scriptural model, I also admit that no one has the corner on the truth. As my grandfather often stated, ***"God never gave anyone all the light."***

Many Independent Baptists who believe they have correctly identified the model, become irritated when they see non-Independent Baptists using rock 'n' roll music, teaching from a Bible other than the King James, sporting casual dress, and claiming to have scores of people genuinely converted by preaching the Gospel of Jesus Christ. Independent Baptists find these churches, which seem to be doing so well, disconcerting—especially when they themselves are struggling to keep 90 members in the church. The answer is not to say, "I'll try a new model with rock music and a different Bible."

One answer is to understand a fundamental truth about the Founder of the local church. In John 12:32 Jesus states, *"And I, if I be lifted up from the earth, will draw all men unto me."* Again, in John 6:44 Jesus says, *"No man can come to me, except the Father which hath sent me draw him: and I will raise him up at the last day."*

There is no doubt in any Bible student's mind that Jesus knew how to draw a crowd. The multitudes followed Him. In fact, He was so successful at drawing the crowds that the religious crowds criticized Him and eventually were able to have Him crucified.

We will talk about criticism later in this book, but we need to understand one clear thought: none of us—**NOT ONE**—is worthy of preaching Christ, nor are we the ***final authority*** on any matter. None of us have it all together. Only pride and its sidekick, insecurity, would challenge those statements.

That being said, let me assert that I do not answer for any church other than the one I pastor. As an Independent Baptist, I believe in soul liberty and personal responsibility. I will answer to Jesus Christ, not for what another pastor did or said, but for what I did and said. Again, this book is not to indict pastors and churches that do not claim to be what we are, but rather to provoke and inspire those who are and those who want to be.

I believe there are false christs, false bibles, and false gospels. Jesus stated in Matthew 7:21,

"Not every one that saith unto me, Lord, Lord, shall enter into the kingdom of heaven...." Again, in Galatians 1:6-8, *"I marvel that ye are so soon removed from him that called you into the grace of Christ unto another gospel: Which is not another; but there be some that trouble you, and would pervert the gospel of Christ. But though we, or an angel from heaven, preach any other gospel unto you than that which we have preached unto you, let him be accursed."* Yes, there are churches that are large and growing and preach a false gospel, but I also believe there are churches which follow contemporary models that have the blessings of God as well.

Allow me to explain. In Revelation 2:18-29, Jesus personally addresses a very hard-working church that is growing and has numerous faults. It is the church of Thyatira. I believe this passage describes many of today's large, contemporary church models.

The church in Thyatira was commended by Jesus for its works, but it was warned to change several significant matters, lest the church see its "children" die. The implication is profound. This growing church did not have a Biblical model that allowed the next generation to sustain its growth. Growth at the expense of the next generation—my, how that describes what is happening today in many large churches. The contemporary tools that brought the crowds into the auditorium allowed the teaching pastor to present the Gospel, but beyond the hearers getting saved, they have received relatively little sound Biblical indoctrination. And the result is that many of that younger generation are leaving those churches, looking for something else.

One can argue that if a church uses the "wrong" Bible, people cannot truly be saved. Practically, that is just plain bogus. Multitudes of us King James believers have used a variety of translations while out soul winning to bring people to Jesus. I have won many Catholics using their own Douay Version. And so have many of you reading this book. I have done the same for Jehovah's Witnesses using their own New World Translation. I am a strong believer in the incorruptible seed (please see my booklet, *Why Stand Against the King James Bible?*), but practically I believe that I can win a soul to Christ without his seeing a Bible. It is the **truth**, not a version, that makes them free.

Again, one can argue that many of these churches today are corrupting the Gospel. Well, the Gospel is clearly defined in I Corinthians 15:1-4, *"Moreover, brethren, I declare unto you the gospel which I preached unto you, which also ye have received, and wherein ye stand; By which also ye are saved, if ye keep in memory what I preached unto you, unless ye have believed in vain. For I delivered unto you first of all that which I also received, how that Christ died for our sins according to the scriptures; And that he was buried, and that he rose again the third day according to the scriptures."* The Gospel is the death, burial, and resurrection of Jesus Christ.

I believe that when a church exalts Jesus Christ as the Son of the Living God and explains the Gospel and makes much of Jesus, God will "draw all men" unto Him. Those who magnify Jesus find favor with God in spite of the issues that may prevent them from having sustained growth after a generation. Thyatira had many faults, including immorality, a female minister, and the "depths of Satan," but God still commended them for their abundant works of church growth. Thyatira sounds like a culturally sensitive church model; nonetheless, God said, *"I know thy works, and charity, and service, and faith, and thy patience, and thy works; and the last to be more than the first."* (Revelation 2:19)

I believe it would be wise for critical Independent Baptists to cast the beam out of their own eyes and set their churches in order according to the Biblical model rather than to scorn those who are exalting Jesus but do not follow completely the correct model. Worse still, some are abandoning the Biblical model and following these "Thyatiran" church models.

As we will emphasize later, many Independent Baptists, plainly and simply, have stopped lifting up and exalting the Saviour; and this, more than anything else, explains why we are in the condition we are today.

Pastor Rick Warren of megachurch fame proclaims, *"It's all about Jesus Christ."* Pastor Warren built his church in contrast to the fact that 7,000 churches in his own denomination (SBC) did not have one convert walk the aisle. The fact that he or others choose to use rock 'n' roll music or another version of the Bible is certainly a valid point of contention, and one which many Fundamental Baptists, including me, would caution as problematic for a man who claims he wants to be both Biblical and relevant; however, a Baptist church isn't blessed simply because Fundamental music or the King James Bible is used. A church is blessed when it promotes Jesus Christ!

Pastor Bill Hybels of Willow Creek Church says,

> As a young adult I rubbed shoulders with people who had spiritual questions: What is the purpose of life? What is beyond the grave? Is Jesus more than a myth? How do I make moral decisions? Is there absolute truth? Does prayer really work? Is there meaning in suffering? They had lots of questions but few answers.
>
> In 1975 a group of friends and I began to call these people "seekers," and we decided to start a church that could reach them—a church that would answer their questions, address their needs, introduce them to Jesus Christ, and give them a taste of His kingdom on earth. We wanted to "be the church" for the people who thought church was irrelevant but who needed it so desperately.[24]

The seeker-sensitive movement was based on answers the community gave in response to a survey. The book *Reveal* shows that the seeker-sensitive model did not bring the desired edification to the church people; therefore, another survey was performed to institute yet another change in the model. That practice is cultural sensitivity—not Scriptural sensitivity.

The correct model is a Scriptural model—not a cultural model. It is a Scriptural model that is as unchanging as the message. Soul winning is not a cultural issue; as a part of the Great Commission, soul winning is a Biblical issue that never changes.

> *"The same things win today that have always won, and they will win years from now. The only difference is the losers have a whole new bunch of excuses why they don't win or can't win."*
> *Paul "Bear" Bryant, one of the winningest coaches in college football history.[25]*

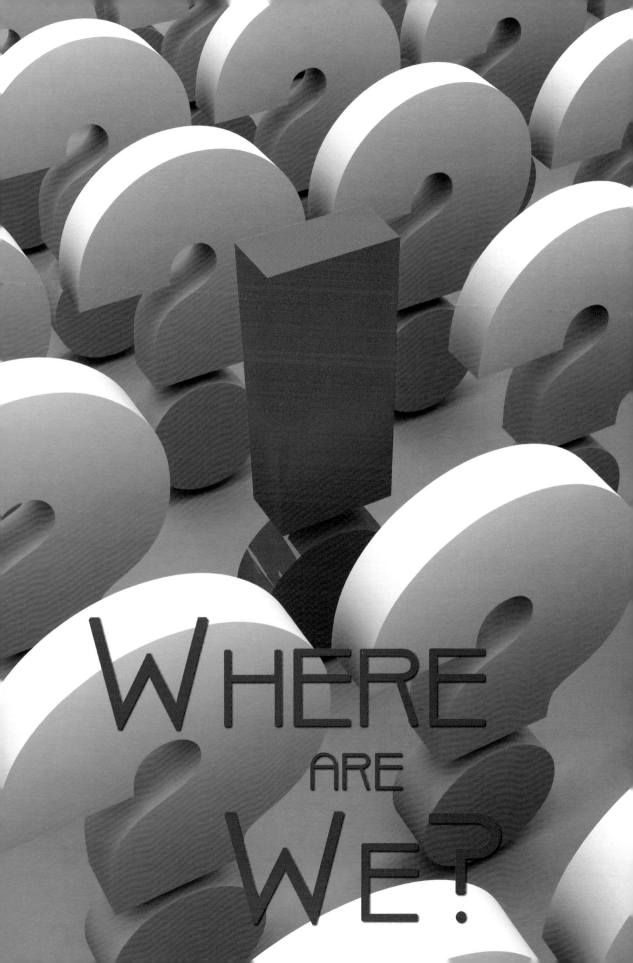

"If we Independent Baptists change as much in the next 33 years as we have changed in the past 33 years, will my grandchildren even recognize what their great-grandfather knew as the old-fashioned Baptist way of church building?"
– Dr. Jack Schaap

CHAPTER ONE

WHERE WE ARE NATIONALLY

The stand that Pastor Jack Hyles led his people to take when pulling out of the American Baptist Convention put First Baptist Church of Hammond in the spotlight, though that attention was not sought. A pastor who had heard about the amazing growth of First Baptist Church called to ask if he could visit and learn how to build his own church. After one week the pastor went home and instituted what he saw at First Baptist Church, and his church began to grow as never before. Others who heard of this pastor's success also expressed a desire to visit First Baptist and learn. Because of this great interest, Pastor Hyles decided to hold a school for pastors.

April 5, 1964, marked the opening day of the first annual Pastors' School, with 167 in attendance. Since that date Pastors' School, which has always been a practical conference, has been a tool to inspire people to help save America. The records of Pastors' School from 30 to 40 years ago record an interesting variety of non-Catholic denominations—Church of Christ, Seventh Day Adventist, Church of God, and United Methodist. From a casual study of Pastors' School, we see that many Christian, non-Catholic denominations looked to Pastors' School as a growth model.

Pastors' School through the years has been the place that has emphasized the Biblical model of aggressive soul winning, discipleship, mentoring, Sunday school, and church growth. There is hardly an area in America where a church does not exist that has in some way been influenced by Pastors' School. Now 45 years old, Pastors' School stands as a strong indicator of the state of Independent Baptists and reveals these churches' alignment.

According to Dr. John Vaughan of *Church Growth Today*:

> ## "50% of churches in America run less than 100, and 80% of churches run less than 200."

In an effort to discover where Independent Baptists stand today, a survey was conducted of approximately 1,100 churches who have sent delegates to one or more Pastors' Schools at First Baptist Church of Hammond, Indiana, since 2001. The 52-percent response rate is well above the national polling average.

The following statistics were gleaned from the Pastors' School attendees' responses to our survey:

Present Sunday Morning Attendance

Pastors' School churches average 240 people in each church on a Sunday morning. Responding churches averaging 100 people or fewer make up 46.2 percent of those surveyed.

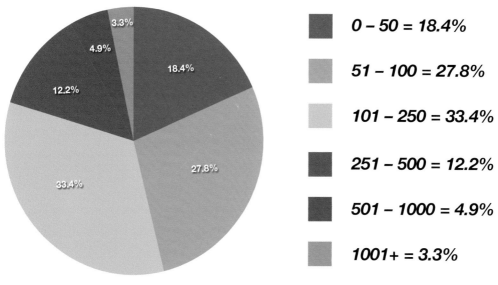

Percentage of Pastors' School Churches Which Average:

- 0 – 50 = 18.4%
- 51 – 100 = 27.8%
- 101 – 250 = 33.4%
- 251 – 500 = 12.2%
- 501 – 1000 = 4.9%
- 1001+ = 3.3%

Bus Ministry

76% of the churches surveyed have a bus ministry.

34.4% of these churches have started their bus ministry since 2001.

80% of these bus ministries average under 100 in attendance.

Tithing

60.1% of the core people in the churches surveyed tithe on a regular basis.

Missions

74.1% of the churches use Faith Promise Giving for missions.

82% of the Pastors' School churches support less than 50 missionaries per church.

According to Fundamental Baptist Missions International, the average church supports a missionary for $76 per month.

GROWTH-RELATED FACTORS

Factoid

36.6% HAVE had to dismiss a key staff member, including, but not limited to, the senior pastor.

57.7% of surveyed churches have experienced a significant number of people leaving at one time.

64% of those churches operating a Christian school started their school before 1979 or after 2000.

63.8% of these churches do not operate a Christian school.

60.4% of the surveyed churches have a discipleship program which mentors new Christians.

Good News!

These Pastors' School churches have experienced a 41% increase in growth between 2000 and 2007!

CHAPTER TWO

A Look Inside the First Baptist Church of Hammond

As part of a look at present-day Independent Baptists, I urged my staff to evaluate our own church and to look at some hard data to allow you the reader to get a better inside look at this megachurch. Not only am I willing to let you see our results, but I encourage other pastors to evaluate their congregations. The Bible encourages us in Proverbs 27:23, *"Be thou diligent to know the state of thy flocks, and look well to thy herds."*

A survey was conducted at First Baptist Church of Hammond during a two-week period in January 2008. From that survey the following facts were learned.

Factoid

MEMBERSHIP & ATTENDANCE

30% of the members of First Baptist Church have become members in the last 5 years.

25% of those who attend our church were reached through the bus ministry.

77% attend services three or more times per week.

Tithes & Offerings

76% tithe on their gross income.

50% give to Faith Promise Missions Giving.

Soul Winning

51% are part of an organized soul-winning ministry at First Baptist Church.

87% have won at least one soul to Christ.

62% say that they regularly witness to two or more people per month about their faith.

Bible Reading

37% of our members spend 15 - 30 minutes per day reading the Bible.

16% of our members spend more than 30 minutes per day reading the Bible.

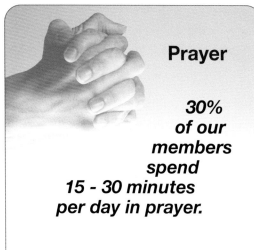

Prayer

30% of our members spend 15 - 30 minutes per day in prayer.

14% of our members spend more than 30 minutes per day in prayer.

When asked what part of the Christian life they would like to improve, the top responses were Bible reading/study, prayer, and soul winning.

How

ARE WE BEING

DISTRACTED?

"I have had two purposes in my entire ministry of seventy-one years. My first purpose has been to win souls. Without Christ, men are lost and Hell-bound. The second purpose of my ministry has been to help Christians grow in grace and become mature, worthwhile servants of our Lord."[1]

– Dr. Lee Roberson

How Are We Being Distracted?

Christ gave us the method and the model and the message. That statement is based on the core essential pillar of all Baptist belief, namely that the Bible is the final authority in all matters of faith and practice. The motto of First Baptist Church of Hammond is, "We Are People of the Book." Two opposing views to the Independent Baptist view are *progressive interpretation*, which means the Bible needs to be continually reinterpreted as new truth is discovered (which is basically the Catholic and the Charismatic philosophy of Bible revelation), and *cultural interpretation*, which is part of the popular modern model stating that because the culture changes, the Scriptures must follow the culture. For instance, many of the most influential models today are considering female pastors, which are patently forbidden in Scripture. It has always been the Baptist position to conform to the Scriptural model, not to conform the Scriptural model to the culture. God would not give His people such an important truth without giving them an example of how truth should be spread. Furthermore, there is both a consensus and confusion among church-growth experts as to which model is successful, along with a tremendous hunger to find any method that will fill the church pews. One of the most recent, oft-copied, contemporary models of church growth in America has admitted a failure in effectively discipling converts to a deeper relationship with Jesus Christ. That admission does not make their model right or wrong, but it does underscore the need to wisely consider what the Biblical model is.

Nearly all Christian groups would agree that a deeper relationship with Jesus Christ is one of their foundational goals. If a comparison were made of Christian models, one would find a strong thread of commonality with that message. What is often the discrepancy is the method and model used.

Some Independent Baptist churches have changed by admitting they are going to follow a different model. Some Independent Baptist churches are still following the correct model, but they are not growing because of the distractions. The main distraction is getting away from lifting up Christ. Those who seem to be getting the job done may not all agree as to each ingredient of the model, but they do have one facet in common—their promotion of Jesus Christ.

It is our contention that a combination of many factors has distracted the Independent Baptist movement, and those distractions have hurt the principal ingredient of the Biblical model, lifting up Jesus Christ. What has taken the Independent, Fundamental Baptists away from promoting Christ since 1976? The following information about possible distractions was researched from surveys and independent study.

MORAL FAILURES

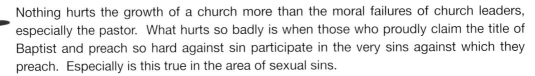

Nothing hurts the growth of a church more than the moral failures of church leaders, especially the pastor. What hurts so badly is when those who proudly claim the title of Baptist and preach so hard against sin participate in the very sins against which they preach. Especially is this true in the area of sexual sins.

- A church in the deep South that was averaging over 5,000 at one time and was the largest church in the state is now running less than 200 due to the pastor's serious moral problem.

- Another church in that same state that had an attendance of over 2,000 is now down to 80 because of the pastor's adultery.

- An Independent Baptist church in the Northeast went from 900 to less than 70 after the pastor had an affair.

- A church in the Midwest dropped from 1,200 to 240 after the pastor's tryst.

- A church in the Southwest that was running almost 1,000 now has less than 500 attending, due to a sordid romantic relationship.

- A church on the West Coast dropped from 2,500 to 600 after the pastor's unfaithfulness.

- A High Plains church that at one time saw over 1,000 in its pews each Sunday, now has less than 100—the reason? The pastor committed adultery.

- A church in the North that one time was approaching an attendance of close to 800 now runs 400 because of the pastor's sexual misconduct.

- A church in the West that at one time was running over 4,000, currently has less than 120 attending, due to the pastor's sexual sin.

- Another church that at one time was running over 4,000 and was considered to be the fastest-growing church in America, now runs about 50 due to a serious moral problem.

- A West Coast church dropped from 700 to 400 because of the pastor's affair.

- This destruction of churches is not just limited to big churches when a moral problem occurs. A church in a small Midwest town that was running over 100 dropped to 11 after the pastor's adultery.

North, South, East, or West—big, small, or midsized—moral failures destroy churches. It seems to take decades for churches to recover, if they ever do, when the pastor has a moral problem.

Baptists may hide their heads in the sand, but the truth is that conservative Christians and Independent Baptists in particular have not dealt well with a huge distraction called moral failures.[2]

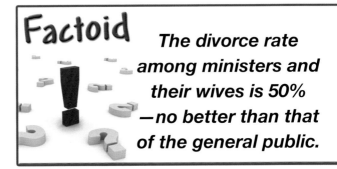

Factoid *The divorce rate among ministers and their wives is 50% —no better than that of the general public.*

> ## *One-third of my counseling is with pastors who are addicted to pornography.*
> – Dr. Tom Williams, Evangelist, Worldwide Ministries, Inc.

The Institute of Church Leadership surveyed 1,050 pastors from across America: 808 (77%) of the pastors surveyed felt they did not have a good marriage; 315 (30%) said they had either been in an ongoing affair or had a one-time sexual encounter with a church member.

In 1985 Richard Blackmon surveyed 1,000 pastors from four major denominations in California. He found that 31.7 percent of the pastors surveyed had sexual intercourse with a church member who was not their spouse.[3]

According to *Time* magazine a recent spate of scandals involving prominent pastors has underscored the challenges their wives face. Eight in ten pastors' wives say they feel unappreciated or unaccepted by their husband's congregations, according to surveys by the Global Pastors' Wives Network (GPWN). The same number wish their husbands would choose another profession. "Wives' issues" is the number-one reason pastors leave their ministries. The divorce rate among ministers and their wives is 50 percent—no better than that of the general public. Loneliness is a running theme among pastors' wives. According to a survey 84 percent of pastors' wives don't feel prepared for their lifestyle. The church becomes the husband's mistress, and the wife loses her identity.[4]

SCHOOLS ─────────────────

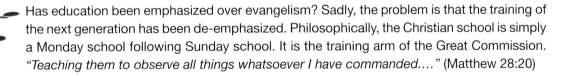

Has education been emphasized over evangelism? Sadly, the problem is that the training of the next generation has been de-emphasized. Philosophically, the Christian school is simply a Monday school following Sunday school. It is the training arm of the Great Commission. *"Teaching them to observe all things whatsoever I have commanded...."* (Matthew 28:20)

The researchers on this particular subject believed that education would be a great distraction in church growth; however, the statistics did not bear out that common misconception. First, 75 percent of churches which were number one in size operated a Christian school. When they discontinued the "Monday school," their church also diminished in size. Christian education could not have been labeled a distraction. Secondly, the researchers discovered that churches with or without schools had equal diminishing attendances. No doubt, some churches became distracted with the demands of a Christian school, but as a movement, statistics indicate that having a Christian school helped boost the church attendance.

Closing the doors to the Christian school is generally an administrative failure. Many a pastor does not realize that his school is not hurting him; it is his inability to administrate that is hurting his church. Those who have Christian schools generally believe it is a fulfillment of the Great Commission. One reason why Fundamentalism is still alive is because of the training of the children. For instance, the whole emphasis in Fundamental Baptist Missions International is for the missionary to start a school as soon as possible in order to teach the heritage of Christianity.

Elmer Towns, in his book *Sunday School and Church Growth*, quotes from the *Journal Champion* as to why many churches stop growing when they begin Christian schools:

> First, it was noted that money was diverted from buses, advertisement, and salary for personnel in evangelism to the school. Second, it was observed that the pastor became a leader of the school, which took time from outreach and pastoring the flock. He became involved in administration and handling discipline problems. Third, promotion became essential. A person can ride only one bicycle at a time, and most pastors can promote only one major project at a time.[5]

A survey of the top 40 churches from the 1976 list found that 75% have, or had, a Christian school. In 2007 only 30% of the top 40 churches operated a Christian school.

LACK OF VISION

How do Disneyland and Disney World rely on teenagers to manage crowds of 60,000 people per day, to keep the place clean, and to make the rides exciting and the experience fun? It's tradition! Specifically, it is the traditions passed on in *"Traditions 101,"* a two-day orientation program. Here, every new employee (even the 90-day summer hires) meet Walt Disney via videotape. They learn about his vision and the underlying values in which every customer is a "guest" and every employee a *"performing artist."* They are quizzed about traditions and come to understand the reason why every rule, policy, and procedure is important.[6]

How did Wal-Mart grow from a small five-and-dime store in Bentonville, Arkansas, to the world's largest retailer in our lifetime? Because one man, Sam Walton, had a vision, and his employees bought into that vision. (One of the significant characteristics of the signature churches was that the pastors had a vision for the church, and the people supported the pastor in his vision.)

In 2005 the people of the First Baptist Church of Hammond, Indiana, were challenged to baptize 25,000 converts in one year. First Baptist Church had been baptizing thousands of converts for many years. One year, over 15,000 had been baptized, but to jump to 25,000 seemed like a huge leap. When one of the assistant pastors asked, "Don't you think we should try for 20,000 first?" he was not prepared for my response. "No, you think you could do 20,000; I want to stretch your faith. Let's go for 25,000." First Baptist Church responded to the challenge by seeing 25,255 converts baptized in one year. When was the last time your faith was stretched?

In our recent Pastors' School survey, it was discovered that 82 percent of those churches surveyed support 50 missionaries or fewer. According to our mission board, FBMI, because of the amount per missionary that the average church gives, the average missionary family needs 88 churches to support him in order that he might actually get to his field of work. Practically speaking, based on the churches that attend Pastors' School, if the average single church's missions giving were given to only one missionary, then 82 percent of our churches would support, at most, 57 percent of one missionary per year. Wow! The average church supports a little over one-half of one missionary.

Diligent work has brought us to the findings that numbers are extremely conflicting. For example, according to *The World Missions Handbook*, in 2006 the total number of Baptist missionaries was just under 10,000. To the contrary, the Southern Baptists show that they currently have over 10,000 missionaries. Other research tells us that there are 29,000 missionaries worldwide. There are two sources that tell us that there are fewer than 2,700 Independent Baptist families on the mission field.

One thing this research has taught me is that we have no way to tell how we are actually doing. I do know what the missionaries abroad are telling me personally. One veteran missionary told me that five missionaries have left his country in the last eight years. Another who served in Russia said that, while there were once 26 or 27 missionaries, currently there are two. Although there are many bright spots, we are unfortunately working very hard at best to tread water.

We are patting ourselves on the back, rejoicing in our mediocrity. We have lost our vision, and truly the people are perishing.

"When I'm through, everyone will have one."
—Henry Ford on the automobile

"There's something going on here, something that is changing the world, and this is the epicenter."
– Steve Jobs during the start-up of Apple Computers

"I believe that this nation should commit itself to achieving the goal, before this decade is out, of landing a man on the moon and returning him safely to the earth."
—President John F. Kennedy, May 25, 1961

"Today's leaders have to be concerned about tomorrow's world and those who will inherit it."[7]

Poor Transfer of Leadership———

Ninety-seven percent of the top 40 churches from the 1976 list have experienced at least one change of pastors. Today only three churches (less than ten percent) in the top 40 still remain in the top 40 listed in 1976. Interestingly, this problem of succession and transfer of leadership is not a new one. In 1949 Dr. Louis Entzminger, the Sunday school superintendent for Dr. J. Frank Norris, published a list of the 25 largest Sunday schools in America. In 1969 when *Christian Life* published its listing of the 50 largest Sunday schools in America, only one of the churches from 1949 remained on the list.

Sadly, the church where Dr. Entzminger and Dr. Norris ministered, the First Baptist Church of Fort Worth—the church that was one of America's early megachurches—is nowhere in sight when the largest churches in America are now listed. In 1928 the church averaged over 5,000 in attendance; current statistics show the church is averaging less than 500 in weekly attendance.

This lack of transfer is not unique to churches. In his book *Why Companies Fail*, Mark Ingebretsen quotes Nancy Bowman-Upton of Baylor University as saying, "Less than one-third of family businesses survive the transition from first- to second-generation ownership. Of those that do, only half survive from second to third generation."[8] In other words, less than 15 percent of businesses make it past three generations![9]

Why is the failure rate so high? Again, quoting from Ingebretsen in his book *Why Companies Fail,* "There should be a succession plan outlining exactly how the transfer of leadership should occur."[10] Why is First Baptist Church of Hammond, Indiana, one of only three and the only Independent Baptist church still on the list of the top 40 churches in America even though it has gone through a change of pastors? High on the list would be that Dr. Jack Hyles had a plan of succession. He had prepared his people for that day when the pulpit would be given to someone else, and today the church is still vibrant. The baton was passed smoothly.

> *A good, strong leader never becomes so weak as when he is going to transition his ministry. He backs off to allow his deacons and the men in his church to have a strong say-so, and when everyone has formed a strong opinion and has become entrenched in his ways, the new man who is voted in does not have a chance. In the First Baptist Church of Hammond, when the strong leader died, immediately the pulpit committee said, "We must put a leader in now." Strong leadership chose a new leader in accordance to plan.*   – Jack Schaap

Not Being Committed

According to studies by Hadaway, Donahue, and Benson in a book called *The Growth and Decline of Congregations,* members of growing churches are more active on average than members of nongrowing churches. Commitment and interest levels are higher. In growing churches, there is a sense that "this is the place to be."

In his book *A Guide to Evangelical Christianity*, David Cobia says, "Contrary to what many think, the average megachurch calls for—and gets—a generally higher level of both personal spiritual commitment and commitment to the church than do other churches."[11]

In my sermon entitled "Where Are We Going in Fundamentalism?" I state that one big reason Fundamental churches have declined is a lack of commitment. They try many models of outreach but are not committed to them. Churches that once had thriving bus ministries no longer run any buses. Churches that once had aggressive soul-winning programs no longer go soul winning.

Larry Smith, an evangelist from St. John, Indiana, who travels to many Independent Baptist churches each year, says that he rarely has a pastor say, "Let's go soul winning." They ask him to go "visiting." They tried soul winning but were not committed, and many of those churches are not growing.

Scott Gray, an evangelist who travels to approximately 35 Baptist churches each year, believes the number-one reason why churches don't grow is that they are constantly changing their ministry. They attend a conference and hear about the bus ministry and try that avenue for a while. They go to another conference and hear about something else, and they try that. With no commitment to the Biblical ways of building a church, there is no growth.

Much is said about the alleged weak convictions of megachurch members and the so-called "watered-down" theology of very large churches. Several indicators from the Hartford Institute's survey seems to indicate otherwise. When asked if the phrase "holds strong beliefs and values" describes the congregation, 78 percent strongly agreed that it did. Additionally, when questioned how much emphasis was placed on home and personal practices, the following was tallied: personal Scripture study strongly emphasized—88 percent, yes; personal prayer or devotions strongly emphasized—86 percent, yes; tithing or sacrificial giving strongly emphasized—78 percent, yes; family devotions strongly emphasized—53 percent, yes.[12]

FINANCES

The laws pertaining to the tax-exempt status of the church should not be taken lightly. Failure to follow a budget or flaunting IRS principles because a church is a nonprofit entity shows both the ignorance and/or the arrogance of the Baptist preacher! The financial liability of a church that does not comply can be devastating. The church needs to stay abreast of and be compliant with IRS code. The pastor should not handle the church's money or sign for any money; he should disassociate himself from the handling of money. The account books should be kept in order and be audit proof.

Three Christian businessmen who are obviously successful in business were asked to share some insights about finances in relation to their heartbeat for God: Joe Wittig, who is a member at First Baptist Church of Hammond, Indiana, and operates several businesses; Dr. Russell Anderson, who has invested in over 480 churches and travels nearly every week of the year to churches; and Dr. Jack DeCoster, who has invested tens of millions of dollars in a variety of Christian ministries. Here are their answers to two important questions:

What makes a church worthy of investment?
- A powerful church (Psalm 111:6; Hebrews 4:12; II Timothy 1:7), one that preaches the Bible (II Timothy 4:2, 3), one that operates by faith, one that is well administrated, one that believes God, and one with many good works (Psalm 11:8)

- A church with a bus ministry and a church with a pastor who has a consistent walk with God, who is on fire in the pulpit, and who brings souls down the aisle

- A faithful church with a proven track record in soul winning (shows production), missions, and good stewardship in the finances of the church and a solid Bible-believing, teaching, and preaching pastor

What practice do you see that hinders church growth?
- A pastor who wears out the seat of his members' britches instead of the soles of his shoes; a pastor who won't get his hands dirty; a pastor who becomes a "superior being"; a pastor who gets lazy; a pastor who delegates away everything; a pastor who takes too many vacations, becomes too "posh," and who pushes his people harder than he pushes himself.

- The pastor, staff, and teachers are not being friendly and aware of visitors, are not following up on visitors, and are unaware of the needs of others.
- Some preachers do not have the head/heart for the big, strong, tough work. These preachers are too laid back and start to let their standards lower. A laid-back worker will not get the work done and will bankrupt the business.

Regarding Finances:
- Be wise with every dollar that the church spends.
- Be open with church members as to where the money is being spent.
- Learn Biblical principles and teach them to the church people.
- Adopt a budget and work diligently to live within that budget.
- Adjust the budget only when necessary.

– Joe Wittig

LET'S EXAMINE A FEW MORE RELEVANT THOUGHTS:

Money and manpower have always been the big needs of the ministry. This directly speaks to the "business" of the ministry. I am afraid far too many young pastors see the ministry as only a "spiritual" entity, and they do not grasp the work that is involved and the business savvy that is vital, be it hiring the right people, training and managing these people, finding the financial resources to care for employees, setting up prudent budgets, managing these budgets, or the thousand other details involved in "God's business."

"Pastors really should not be involved in setting their salaries and determining what types of cars the ministry should provide them and various other perks. A most uncomfortable situation is deal[ing] with the founder of a ministry who still runs the day-to-day operations and is accustomed to making all decisions and asking no one for permission to do anything. In these worst-case scenarios there is usually no accountability, no financial disclosure, and most often, a degree of corruption by the world. Those who continue to handle financial accountability and transparency via "seat of the pants" approach are looking for trouble. Being too close to large sums of money is too much of a temptation for most men and women. Those who are wise will seek the counsel of others and find ways to separate themselves from that which would cause them to stumble."[13]

Many pastors downplay and even criticize the business model of the ministry; yet, the unspeakable failure of God's churches to succeed at the Great Commission only screams at those pastors who smugly hide their business ignorance behind their self-perceived spirituality.

There is no dichotomy between spirituality and business mindedness. Church work is people work, and it is money work. Ninety-eight percent of what a pastor of a large and growing church does is nearly identical to what a CEO of a small to midsize business does. Bible researchers state that one of every five verses in the Bible addresses the issue of money, and the pastor who ignores that condemns his ministry to staying relatively small and ineffective. What many pastors fail to understand is that God is a tough and demanding Businessman. Just look at the parables Jesus told in the Gospels. The examples abound of God's expecting a good return on His investment and doling out harsh judgment on the lazy and unproductive.

Church analysts tell us that 95 percent of all church failures are directly related to the pastor's inability to administrate. According to the Bible, administration is a spiritual gift given to men. Churches that dismiss this ability as relatively unimportant condemn their church's future growth.

I have never known a church or a pastor to fail due to weak preaching, but I have counseled scores of churches who have a pastor who is strong in the pulpit but inept in business. In fact, some of the largest Baptist churches I have known are pastored by average pulpiteers but men who are wise administrators.

Independent Baptists are quite vocal about their love for good preaching but rarely testify about the business savvy of their pastors. So, what we find again and again within the circles of Fundamentalism is an inspirational ministry that measures success by the crowd at the invitation altar only and not by the stability of the corporate body of believers or by the spiritual stability of well-grounded believers. Apparently, if a man does not know how to manage and lead people and he does not know much of anything about business and finance, but he can holler in the pulpit and tell a tear jerker of a story, then he is eminently qualified to be the senior pastor, bishop, and elder of a New Testament local church. In my opinion, that is Biblical ignorance and ministerial homicide.

Those three Bible words—*pastor, bishop, elder*—establish the full responsibility of a senior church leader.

- Pastor = (Greek word transliterated is *poimain*) implies a shepherd leading his flock and relates to the teaching and training responsibility.

- Bishop = (Greek word transliterated is *episkapos*) addresses the business of the church. The word refers to one who is capable of managing other workers and job assignments.

- Elder = (Greek word transliterated is *presbuteros*) refers to the mature spiritual leadership and the counseling aspect of a minister, implying one who is able to perfect or mature the saints. It also speaks to the need of exhortation and the training of the next generation.

The ministry of the Christian Law Association is contacted in excess of 100,000 times annually. On average they will be contacted by over 1,200 different churches each month with all forms of legal or other ministry distractions vying for the attention of the church's leadership.

Some of the key distractions that church leaders contact our attorneys about break down on average as follows:

- *Child abuse issues – 25%*

- *Financial issues or problems in the church – 25%*

- *Christian school and land use issues – 20%*

- *Litigation (both threatened and actual) – 15%*

- *Leadership/staff/board tension – 15%*

Financial Accountability

by Rick Finley, Pastor
Fellowship Baptist Church, Durham, North Carolina

In 1988 I became the pastor of a rather large and influential church. Not long after assuming the office, I realized that the organizational and procedural policies of the ministry left much to be desired. The church had no bylaws, and the financial structure was subpar. There were many different checking accounts in existence. Accountability was not what it should have been. I began to make adjustments, but after more than three decades under my predecessor's leadership, the people were very slow to change. A little less than four years into my ministry as pastor, it became apparent that I should have pushed harder for change.

As is the case with any new pastor, some people did not accept my leadership. Folks began to question decisions that I was making. I was accused of being dictatorial and cultish. Although it was a small remnant of people, they were people who were in positions of leadership under the former administration, so they knew our weaknesses. Suddenly, people began to question the financial propriety of our ministry. They began to question the multiple checking accounts. They asked if I had purchased a new suit for each of our two assistant pastors. When I told them that I had, they asked if the church had voted on these expenditures. When I told them that the deacons had approved the purchases, they asked for the minutes of the deacons' meetings, knowing full well that the church had not kept minutes from these meetings in decades.

Opposition began to grow, and accusations ran rampant. I was accused of embezzling $40,000. "Misappropriation of funds" were words that were used by our opposition relentlessly. The local television station was contacted, and reporters began calling my home and our office, wanting the "inside scoop" on the story. For two days every newscast included photographs of our church emblazoned with the word "embezzlement." The disgruntled members hired an attorney who demanded that his clients be granted access to all the financial records of the church. My personal finances were audited by our state Department of Revenue. The conflict came to a head at a specially called business meeting on a Thursday night, and after more than three hours of heated discussion, 300 people left our church.

It took years for our ministry to recover. Families were divided, people were hurt, and our work for God suffered a setback that was extremely difficult to overcome. The financial practices were not the cause of the revolt. Our failures were simply solid ground upon which the enemy could secure sure footing.

The Importance of
Committed Followship————

A well-known pastor in the 70s and 80s, who pastored in the mid-South, was recognized as a premier leader in Fundamental circles. His church, which was averaging over 2,000, built a new auditorium; however, in a matter of a few years, the church floundered and disbanded. It was a devastating blow to another large Independent Baptist church. Many of his contemporaries theorized that he went under because he overbuilt. The pastor was kind enough to share with me what really happened at his former church as a valuable insight for me as our church in Hammond was entering a $25-million building program. He explained that his church was divided under his leadership, and in an attempt to bring unity, he decided to build a building. The people who were not committed to his leadership felt they were being forced into a building program, so they withdrew their support. The committed people could not sustain the payments.

The church was in a building program and needed to borrow almost $500,000 to complete the project. The church family was interested in supplying the bond money for the project, instead of a conventional loan but needed to go through an official bond company. They chose a company called Fidelity that had handled general obligation bonds before and was currently handling hundreds of Baptist churches. Some of the largest Baptist churches in America were using this company.

The Federal Securities Commission wanted to investigate Fidelity because they were not a part of the government's bonding companies. The investigation eventually turned up no irregularities but tied up the monies and the paybacks for several years. Since the bonds were issued to church members and they could not get paid as they were promised, many left the church.

The pastor said it was devastating to the attendance of the church, as well as many of the other larger churches. The adverse publicity and the enormous cost eventually caused the collapse of Fidelity Bond Company. The event demoralized the congregation and stunted future growth for years and eventually caused the church to disband.

When I heard this story and other stories like it decades ago, I determined in my heart that should the day come when I pastored and needed to expand, I would only do so with a hundred-percent commitment from the church leadership and deacon board and that the deacons would help to "sell" the idea to the people. It would not be "my" idea, but rather "all our idea."

> **The folks who attend megachurches not only attend, but they support them. The average megachurch budget is $6 million per year. That budget supports a typical staff of 20 to 25 pastors and additional 30 to 50 administrative staff.**[14]

LOSS OF FOCUS
THE "BLUE LIGHT" DIMS

How did Kmart go from a company that had eclipsed Sears as the nation's largest retailer in the 1980s to a company that would file for bankruptcy in 2002? According to *Fortune Magazine* writer Jerry Useem, they fell victim to the "strategy du jour." He says that Kmart embraced the "whatever quick fix" ideology that seemed popular at the time.[15]

At one point, Kmart's customers were as loyal as Wal-Mart customers are today, yet they lost their focus. When a company loses sight of what business it is in, it loses its business. When a church loses sight of what business it is in, it soon loses its church.

In Luke 2:49 Jesus said, *"…wist ye not that I must be about my Father's business?"* The only place where the kingdom work of God is described as a business is from the lips of the Founder of the church. Oftentimes, those who mention the church as being a business are strongly criticized by others as being unspiritual and unscriptural! People who do not study business fall victim to not understanding the business of the church. The church has to adopt the standards that Jesus set in the Word of God and then work diligently on how to market that standard to the community. The church does not ask the community how they should build their product. Reaching and evangelizing the world is only part of the business of a church. The church must also practice sound financial practices and strong financial fundraising, hiring practices, and policy practices for its staff, as well as codes of ethics or conduct for the church layleadership.

The business model is always "Know your product." Before you know your customers, you had better know your product. You only know the customer to the degree that you are trying to approach them with the product. You don't study the customer base and decide, I'm going to make cars. You make cars, and you abide by policies that govern how you make cars—tires, chassis, etc. You market in a certain way to the public so they know you have this product, but the product is designed according to set standards.

Churches should define their business as "Excellence defined by Christ" and continually work to raise the church to the business excellence and standard of what Christ established.

> *"The Great Commission is emphasized in Matthew, Mark, Luke, John, and Acts—five times the last Words of Jesus Christ were emphasized. How many times does He have to give His last Words before we realize this is important? The focus is the Great Commission."*
> –Dr. Jack Schaap

IMBALANCE OF ISSUES

The Christian Coalition, Moral Majority, Family Research Council, Pro-life, and Concerned Women of America are just a few of the political action groups with whom Fundamental Christians and, in particular Independent Baptists, have become involved. It needs to be stated that the Moral Majority movement helped Ronald Reagan win the Presidency, was instrumental in helping to elect two conservative people to the Supreme Court, and aided in bringing about a resurgence of conservative Christian values in America. Christians still enjoy the benefits of that resurgence of acceptability of the conservative right. Though the Moral Majority did hurt the Fundamental movement, it also brought about a renaissance of acceptability of the movement. The Moral Majority made it respectable for Christians to discuss politics and other critical social issues. However, there are no flawless movements. When the Fundamentalists saw some of their own closing ranks with these groups, they knee jerked and said the Moral Majority was bad, when in actuality, it gave them credibility. Suddenly, men like Jerry Falwell were no longer "dumb Fundamentalists."

Christians are supposed to be salt in the community; they are supposed to flavor their communities. Working with city and state officials, praying for them, and honoring them is a part of reaching out in the community. It is also part of the command Paul gave to Timothy in I Timothy 2:1-4. To deny that is to limit the outreach of the church. However, the problem was that several ordained pastors were leaving their pulpits to become political activists. Instead of embracing the Moral Majority by finding some laymen in the church to help in their political endeavors, the pastor left his focus—prayer and the ministry of the Word. What really destroyed some Independent, Fundamental Baptist churches was undue criticism of each other. Pastors all over America began naysaying the Moral Majority when that was not the issue: the real issue was imbalance and becoming singular in focus.

Interestingly, all of these political action groups have either started or have come to prominence since 1976. Many of the churches that were on the top 100 list in 1976 became involved with these kinds of organizations. Today those churches are no longer on the list of the top 100. That's interesting.

A church that was in the top 20 in 1976 became involved in a tax fight with the U.S. government. A few years ago the IRS seized the church's buildings and property, and they were left without a place to meet. Was the church right? Well, they may have believed that their cause was right; but, now they are dead right! Let me add this: It is certainly up to a church as to what causes they want to address. But if entering into a fracas causes a church to diminish or stop its fulfillment of the Great Commission, that church needs to put the brakes to whatever it is fighting and go back to the book of Acts to reset the button on its ultimate mission and commission.

The perceived political involvement of the megachurch indicates they are bigtime players when it comes to politics and social issues. However, a survey by the Hartford Institute for Religion Research paints a different picture. The survey conducted in 2005 found that megachurches tend to be conservative. Of the 1,200 surveyed churches, 50 percent claimed to be predominately conservative; 33 percent said that they were somewhat conservative; 11 percent chose middle of the road; 4 percent were somewhat liberal, and 2 percent selected liberal. Surprisingly, only 16 percent of the surveyed churches said that they had partnered with other churches in political involvement activities in the past five years, and 76 percent said that they had never done so.[16] Yes, the present-day megachurch is conservative in nature, but it is not focused on political activities.

The rate of growth of megachurches strongly correlates with the reported absence of conflict in the congregation. Those churches that grew by the greatest percentage also experienced the least amount of major conflict, and conversely those that experienced no growth or an actual decline in attendance had the greatest rates of major conflict.

Grouping by Growth Rates:[17]

Has the church had conflicts or disagreements in past 2 years?	No growth or decline	1 to 20% growth	21 to 50% growth	51 to 100% growth	More than 100% growth
No conflict I am aware of	9.1%	50.0%	50.%	56.1%	66.7%
Some minor conflict	60.6%	38.9%	43.3%	50.2%	33.3%
Major conflict	30.3%	11.1%	6.7%	3.7%	0%

The churches' major failure in regard to politics is to not follow the admonition of I Timothy 2, which says that the Christian's relationship with his political leadership is to supplicate, pray, intercede, and give thanks. Too many Christians fail to see our government officials as fellow servants; the Bible calls them "ministers of God." Christians fail to understand that God rules in the affairs of men. Christians have jumped into politics in an unscriptural zone instead of following the Scripture. City Hall is not the enemy, but neither should it be the focus of the church's mission.

> *"Church growth is hurt when the leader becomes distracted by criticism and feels he has to defend himself. Church growth is also hurt when the leader draws his followers into professional wars. Professional leaders will disagree, but their followers should not be drawn into that conflict. Management and union leaders have strong debates, but the company is not hurt until the disagreement escalates into a strike when the followers are drawn into the fray. Then the dissension hurts the customers; nobody wins."*

King James Bible Controversy

Allow me to wade into a treacherous stream with strong currents and multiple hidden dangers; however, it is one that illustrates well the distractions that have hurt the Independent Baptist church-growth movement. The King James Bible issue is a good example of what sidetracked many Fundamental Independent Baptists. Because of the sensitivity my Baptist brethren have on this issue, let me state here that I am unequivocally a "King-James" man. There is so much misinformation and disinformation being written and spoken on the matter, however, that a calm and intelligent discussion on the subject is nearly impossible; at least it was in the 80s and 90s.

The issue is significant and demands that every student of God's Word be instructed in the theological definitions of *revelation, inspiration, illumination, and preservation.* Because of the amount of "foolishness" being bantered about on this subject by careless Bible students, such as teaching that the King James Version is inspired, we have "shot ourselves in the foot" in the eyes of many who sincerely seek to understand our position but look askance at us when we prove we ourselves do not understand the issue.

Recently, I read an article that concerned me in a publication from a well-known Independent Baptist church that also operates a Bible college. The article was written by the church's youth pastor, who is a graduate of another Bible college. The article concerned me because a statement was made that the King James Bible is inspired by God.

Because of the perception that this church and college are academically minded and theologically sound, it is all the more disconcerting that such a statement would be made in one of their official publications. But the statement is symptomatic of the confusion on this issue, which is representative of much of the confusion in many of the debates that ripple through our ranks of Fundamentalism.

Simply stated, the King James Bible is a translation. Those of us who have extensively studied the subject understand that God inspired the Hebrew and Aramaic and Greek manuscripts that are often referred to as "the originals." In other words, those of us who believe that *"All scripture is given by inspiration of God"* believe that God breathed out or spoke the very words of Scripture to the various human authors who penned the words that God gave them. God did this in a variety of ways—some by direct conversation, as in the case with Moses; some by writing the words Himself and then giving those words to a man, again as in the case with the Ten Commandments to Moses; and others by a vision, as in the case of many of Ezekiel's writings. The point being, God Himself spoke or gave or "inspired" the very words of the original works of Scripture.

Regarding the King James Version, I do not believe that God spoke the English words to the writers of Hampton Court in the years 1604-1611. But I do believe that the same God Who spoke, or inspired, the originals, worked by His sovereignty through Divine providence to preserve His words in the English language so that what those men gave to the world in 1611 was an accurate and complete record of God's Word in the English language. Now, for you technical worriers out there, we understand that there were more than 20,000 errors of spelling and typesetting in the first edition of the 1611 King James Bible. These errors and the changes of spelling were corrected over the course of years, and the 1881 Scrivener's edition that has been used by Cambridge Press is generally regarded as the most accurate edition.

For one to believe that God inspired the King James Version of the Bible, he would be espousing Catholic or charismatic theology. Both groups theologically believe that God can and does still "speak" today, either through the papal office "ex cathedra," or by way of "a word of knowledge," supposedly used to more perfectly and accurately pronounce and define God's will for man. Kindly put, that theological position is heresy to those of us who believe that the Words of Scripture were ended with the completion of John's finished manuscript of The Revelation approximately 95-100 A.D.

I am confident that the youth pastor who wrote that the King James Version is inspired does not fully understand the error of his wording. And I know that his pastor does not hold to a Catholic or charismatic theology. But it is those kinds of careless wordings that make good people searching for the truth and those within our ranks who know better to become frustrated and distracted by the issue.

This issue is a "hot-button" issue. Just mention the topic to a crowd of Fundamentalists, and the roars and vocalizations will be astounding. You are either with them or against them, and no amount of reasoning is going to persuade them from what they do not know. My point in this article is not to reopen the controversy, though I delighted to teach the subject in college and would happily answer sincere queries on the matter.

My point is to say this: Churches and pastors who were changing versions of the Bible and were leaving the King James Version position were also leaving the Biblical model for church building. They were changing their music, their style of worship service, their standards of dress, their philosophy on soul winning; stopping their bus ministries; and attending other colleges and conferences to conform to a cultural model. In other words, the King James Version crowd was making it an issue of "Which version?" when that issue was only part of the larger question, "Who are you, and where do you think you are going?" We could better have asked them, "Are you following the world's model or the Biblical model?" "Which version?" would have come later. First, let's decide if we even believe the Bible to be our Final Authority. We were arguing about "symptoms" but not addressing the disease.

The pastors and churches who believed the King James Version-only position still believe that today, and those who did not believe it 20 years ago, do not believe it today. We spent vast amounts of time and resources convincing ourselves of something we already believed and still believe. We only succeeded in saying many unkind things about each other, suspicioning each other, and alienating a multitude of younger pastors who had been looking to us for a role model and leadership but became confused and disenchanted with our near barbarism. Cursing, swearing, name calling, and character assassination were all considered fair play in order to "defend God's Word."

But God's Word did not need defending; it needed obedience. If we had used the King James Version to build strong, soul-winning, thoroughly indoctrinated churches, our works would have been all the answer that was needed. The proof is in the pudding, not in the argument. We could not shut our mouths long enough to get the work done, and so the work floundered while our mouths and our pens were in overdrive. As Dr. Hyles was often inclined to say, "Don't defend your weapon; just use it. That will answer the critic."

Certainly, any wise pastor or college dean will thoroughly instruct his flock and his students in the complex study of critical thinking relative to Biblical integrity and the modern attacks against both inspiration as well as preservation. But one does not destroy the work of God in the name of defending the Word of God, any more than one destroys his church defending his right to interpret constitutional tax codes by his conscience. That, as they say, is a "no-brainer."

CRITICISM

In his book *Exceeding Customer Expectations*, Kirk Kazanjin says people stop doing business with a company for six primary reasons:

1. One percent die.
2. Three percent move away.
3. Five percent develop other relationships.
4. Nine percent leave for competitive reasons.
5. Fourteen percent are dissatisfied with the product.
6. Sixty-eight percent go elsewhere because of the poor way they were treated by the employees of the company.

The author states, *"Successful retention, therefore, means building personal relationships with customers with the goal of keeping them for life."*[18] Any salesman will maintain that repeat customers are the lifeblood of any business.

Factoid

From a survey conducted by the Institute of Church Leadership Development, 3,803 people were asked, "Why did you leave the church?" Sixty-one percent left because of a conflict with another member, resulting from gossip or strife that would not stop, was not true, or was not properly dealt with.[19]

I double-dog dare you to find an Independent Baptist who lived through the 80s and 90s who does not think we greatly hurt our movement by the foolish and unwarranted criticism made by "the brethren" toward "the brethren." Quite bluntly, we magnified men—either by criticizing them or semiworshipping them—above the Lord Jesus Christ.

Brethren, we are called to "PREACH CHRIST." And trying to figure out whether another man is worthy or unworthy to preach is absolute foolishness and gross immaturity. And it is near idolatrous to make any one man the litmus test as to whether another man is a worthy Fundamentalist on the basis of his perceived loyalty to that man. The Scriptures warn about those who put their trust in men or in princes. Our trust must be in the Lord.

I greatly fear that the Independent Baptist crowd is still *"biting and devouring one another,"* and we should beware *"...lest we are consumed one of another."* We have become self-styled experts in critiquing, criticizing, and destroying our testimonies, our sermons, our books, our works, and one another. I am so terribly embarrassed at the way we have disrespected one another, I fear to meet my Saviour without wondering what shame we have caused Him and the most precious work He entrusted to our care.

Our movement has far too many insecure and Biblically ignorant men working their jaws and their pens of judgment. We are better than that, gentlemen. Our cause and our work and our calling and our LORD are all worthy of much more than we are giving them, and they are worthy of our treating each other with the honor and respect and humility that our vocation demands.

I do not have much hope of silencing the barking dogs of Fundamentalism, but I would like to give some brief thoughts to those who are on the receiving end of the wagging tongues.

Criticism may come to the leader for four reasons:
An excerpt from *Servant Leadership* by Pastor Jack Schaap

- Criticism serves as a reminder that we are accountable and responsible for what we say and do. The word *responsible* means "able to respond or to give an answer." Being responsible is a willingness to say, "I gave the answer. I said it, and I will stand behind my words."

- Criticism should humble us, as it reminds us of the greatness of our work as Christians and our own personal unworthiness. A tremendous man who was being criticized about being unworthy to preach and to pastor his church called me for advice.

After I listened to him, I simply asked, "Are you worthy?"

"When you put it that way, Brother Schaap, no, not really," he replied and then added, "Are you worthy to pastor your church?"

"No," I answered. "The critics are right—you are not worthy! I am not worthy! No one is truly worthy. Criticism is a reminder that nobody is worthy to preach the unsearchable riches of Christ."

Criticism reminds us that we are not worthy to be called *Christians*—"Christ ones." Criticism should humble us, because we know how unworthy we are. We are just sinners saved by grace.

- Criticism should convict us of the incredible injustice God receives at the hands and mouths of mankind. As disappointing and hurtful as criticism is to us, how much more so must it be for a holy and righteous God to receive it? After all, what has God done to deserve any criticism? For the God Who created the heavens and the earth in six days to listen to the pathetic excuses for humanity to demand their rights, threaten to do what they want to do, and refuse to obey Him is incomprehensible!

Criticism reminds me that God never deserves a negative thought. *"From the rising of the sun unto the going down of the same the LORD's name is to be praised."* (Psalm 113:3) And when we don't praise His name, what a high offense that must be to Him! Romans 3:23 says, *"For all have sinned, and come short of the glory of God."* What is the sin that we commit? We fail to give glory to God. This verse means that if we fail to give glory to God, we have committed an egregious sin.

We call those who smoke and drink and curse sinners, but these do not constitute the "great" sin; the great sin is not giving God the glory due Him! But God is patient—even though we do not deserve His patience.

- Criticism reminds us that we are responsible not only for what we say, but in many respects, we are also accountable for what people think we said. That is painful. Real maturity says, "I am sorry that you misunderstood my words. I apologize because that is not what I intended." A real man (or a real woman) apologizes and properly restates the thought in understandable words and language that properly conveys his heart.

The unfavorable judgment and disapproval of our fellowmen is never easy to endure; however, the one who lives with criticism joins ranks with the Greatest Leader Who ever lived—Christ. Like Jesus, the leader learns to live above the criticism of others.

> *Our cause and our work and our calling and our LORD are all worthy of much more than we are giving them, and they are worthy of our treating each other with the honor and respect and humility that our vocation demands.*

INADEQUATE LEADERSHIP ─────────────

You have heard it before, "Everything rises and falls on leadership," but it is true. Sam Walton turned serving customers into an empire by getting his employees to tap their natural good feelings toward fellow human beings. He made his associates feel that what they were doing was worthwhile. He led them to treat customers in a friendly and helpful way, which built customer loyalty and thus advantage.

The Enterprise Car Rental Company operates in an industry littered with countless failures; yet, this company has recorded impressive gains each year for the past five decades. How? Perhaps because its founder, Jack Taylor, laid out a simple yet effective philosophy, "Take care of your customers and employees, and the profits will follow."[20] Enterprise has an unbending determination to keep its customers happy—whatever it takes. Their goal is to exceed the customers' expectations.

Inadequate leadership is not someone stepping up and saying, "I want to be the head of the movement." Inadequate leadership goes back to the fact that a predominant number of Baptist pastors don't see the big picture. It is not that Independent Baptist churches need a Jack Taylor or a Sam Walton; the average Baptist church needs a leader.

If one takes a careful look at the list of churches from 1976, many were pastored by dynamic, visionary leaders who were the movers and shakers of their day among soul-winning churches. Some of these men found a model that brought them overnight recognition and success. However, financial failures, moral failures, marital failures, and other crises began to erode the leadership ability of these men. That kind of leadership is not what is needed today.

When asked the question, "What are the particular temptations of ministries today?" by *Christianity Today*, Warren Wiersbe responded:

> One of the greatest temptations for the younger preacher today is the yearning for instant success. There are dozens of books on how to dress for success, how to preach, pray, manage, and motivate for success. Because of the media and mega ministries, people are success conscious. Young ministers are tempted to be more concerned about reputation than character. As a consequence, they may take shortcuts and may spend a lot of time trying to imitate somebody else instead of being themselves, developing their own character, their own unique ministry. We have a tendency to want the quick fix. I'm concerned when somebody says, "It worked at Willow Creek; it will work for us in Lincoln, Nebraska."

> Some of the young men have not taken time to discover the past. Because of that, they don't last too long. My generation was taught to study preaching. We know how F. W. Robertson would deal with a text, how Spurgeon would deal with it, how Jowett would deal with it. From studying the great preachers, we learned that each preacher is himself. If you handed me five sermons of great preachers, I could come close to identifying who preached them without reading the byline.

> Also, reading great preaching arouses the imagination. You realize that one text can be approached in hundreds of ways. To me it's reassuring and exciting to find out that preaching is not just mechanics, but art.[21]

Every church needs a pastor who will study the model, preach the message, and institute the proper methods. Not every pastor is a pattern pastor, but every pastor can follow the Biblical model. Not every church has the opportunity to become a pattern ministry, but every church can copy the Biblical example. Nobody would deny that some of today's megachurch pastors are pace setting, cutting-edge, fabulous leaders. Fortune 500 companies would agree that many of them are courageous, bold, daring, and willing to admit mistakes.

What is desperately needed in the church leadership arena are some courageous Bible pastors who will believe and look to the book of Acts and identify pattern ministries copying that Bible model and say, "Our church needs to return to what it's supposed to be doing." That responsibility is following the Great Commission! It is not only Independent Baptists' responsibility; it is every church's responsibility.

> According to Hartford Institute, there is no doubt that the senior pastor is the key component in the success of the megachurch. From their 2005 survey, 83 percent of the churches have seen dramatic growth during the tenure of the current pastor. The typical megachurch pastor is 50 years old and well-educated (92 percent have a college degree or higher; 35 percent hold a doctoral degree).[22]

"Prayer is not necessarily for us to get God's blessings. It is given so that we can get to know God." – Jack Schaap

LACK OF PRAYER

Acts 6:4, *"But we will give ourselves continually to prayer, and to the ministry of the word."*

There are untold causes and issues and duties to which the pastor can "give" himself; but, as Jesus succinctly said in Luke 10:42, *"But one thing is needful: and Mary hath chosen that good part, which shall not be taken away from her."* What was Mary doing? She was sitting at the feet of Jesus. Brethren, we have given ourselves to every good and not-so-good cause. But one thing is needful!

Pastors today are faced with more work, more problems, and more stress than at any other time in the history of the church. This is taking a frightening toll on the ministry, shown by the following North American statistics:

- Fifteen hundred pastors leave the ministry each month due to moral failure, spiritual burnout, or contention in their churches.

- Eighty percent of pastors and eighty-four percent of their spouses feel unqualified and discouraged in the pastorate.

- Fifty percent of pastors are so discouraged that they would leave the ministry if they could, but have no other way of making a living.

- Eighty-five percent of pastors said their greatest problem is they are sick and tired of dealing with problem people, such as disgruntled elders, deacons, worship leaders, worship teams, board members, and associate pastors. Ninety percent said the hardest thing about ministry is dealing with uncooperative people.

Pastors' Wives:
- Eighty percent of pastors' spouses feel their spouse is overworked.

- Eighty percent of pastors' wives feel left out and unappreciated by the church members.

- Eighty percent of pastors' spouses wish their spouse would choose another profession.

- Eighty percent of pastors' wives feel pressured to do things and be something in the church that they are really not.

Pastors' Relationship With the Lord:
- Seventy percent of pastors do not have a close friend, confidant, or mentor. Ninety-five percent of pastors do not regularly pray with their spouses.

- Eighty percent of pastors surveyed spend less than 15 minutes a day in prayer.

- Seventy percent said the only time they spend studying the Word is when they are preparing their sermons.

  [These statistics came from across denomination lines and have been gleaned from various reliable sources such as *Pastor to Pastor, Focus on the Family, Ministries Today, Charisma Magazine, TNT Ministries, Campus Crusade for Christ,* and the *Global Pastors Network*.]

According to a study released by Ellison Research on May 23, 2005, only 16 percent of Protestant ministers across the country are very satisfied with their personal prayer life. Another 47 percent are somewhat satisfied with it. Thirty percent are somewhat dissatisfied, and seven percent are very dissatisfied with their prayer life.

The average Protestant minister prays for 39 minutes a day, although 21 percent spend 15 minutes or less per day in prayer. Younger ministers average 35 minutes a day in prayer, compared to 41 minutes among pastors 45 to 59 years old, and 38 minutes among older pastors.

What defines pastors who are satisfied with their prayer lives versus those who are not?
- The amount of time spent in prayer: Pastors who are very satisfied spend an average of 56 minutes a day in prayer; those who are somewhat satisfied average 43 minutes; those who are somewhat dissatisfied average 29 minutes; and those who are very dissatisfied average 21 minutes.

- How they divide their prayer time: Ministers who are very satisfied spend considerably less time than average making requests, and considerably more time in quiet time or listening to God.

- What they pray for: The more satisfied ministers are with their prayer life, the more likely they are to spend time praying for "big issues" beyond their own lives and churches—overseas missions, local outreach and evangelism efforts, other local churches and pastors, the country as a whole, individual Christian leaders, individual government leaders.[23]

> *"Many people have a prayer time; few people have a prayer life."*
> – Dr. Tom Williams

> *"Everyone wants to give prayer a polite nod."*
> – Dr. David Gibbs, Jr.

LACK OF INNOVATION———————————

Just about everyone has heard of Henry Ford, the revolutionary innovator in the automobile industry and a legend in American business history. He had a vision to put the automobile within the reach of the average American, and with his Model-T, he did. By 1914 Ford was producing 50 percent of all automobiles in the United States.

However, all of Ford's story is not about achievement. Henry Ford was so in love with his Model-T that he never wanted to change it or improve it. For almost 20 years, Ford Motor Company offered only one design, the Model-T, in one color, black. It wasn't until 1927 that he finally grudgingly agreed to offer a new car to the public, the Model-A. By then it was too late! The competitors were far ahead of Ford in technical innovations, and by 1931 Ford was down to 28% of the market.

In recent years the Japanese have done the same to the "Big 3" automakers. While Detroit has hung on to the same old plans and procedures, Honda and Toyota have become the best-selling cars in America.

Could it be that the Independent Baptist churches in America are a picture of Henry Ford and the United States' auto industry? In Elmer Towns' book *11 Innovations in the Local Church: How Today's Leaders Can Learn, Discern, and Move Into the Future,* he states, "Innovation or death. Too many churches choose death over innovation. The choice we make today will impact the church of our children."[24]

Innovations do matter—but without compromise!

Every theologian or philosophical historian credits the rapid rise in Christianity during the first century with:

- The Roman system of peace. The Apostle Paul, who was freeborn, was a citizen of Rome, and the citizens of Rome were protected, so Paul could freely travel anywhere in the Roman Empire.

- The Roman system of paved roads was a modern wonder.

- The Greek language and the Greek culture. The universal language of Greek made communicating the Gospel immeasurably easier than having to learn each country's unique language or dialect. The Greek culture taught a questioning mind; as a result, the people were willing to question old-standard idolatrous practices and to listen to Christianity's early missionaries. These early innovations in the Roman Empire opened the door to the spread of Christianity.

In D. L. Moody's day, a question arose over whether or not the innovative horseless carriage should be adopted, or should they remain with the reliable horse and buggy. People who were considered conservative probably called that choice "modernistic," when it was merely a matter of technology used as a tool. People did not understand

> **If Jesus could walk on water, why did He step in a boat to teach?**

modernism—man's attempt to water down doctrine in order to make it more palatable to man. Innovation has often been considered the brother of modernism, a designation used by preachers and evangelists in the late 50s. When researching the true intent and meaning of the term *modernism*, like many definitions, it has changed with time. The modernism against which men of God like W. B. Riley preached, embraced liberalism, evolution, and other issues that were in direct defiance to Biblical doctrines. The change in the church's Biblical teaching, standards, and even the Bible itself were the true evidence and meaning of modernism.

If it is wrong to use I-MAG screens, television, radio, and billboards, then it is also wrong to use padded pews, public address systems, tracts, air-conditioning, jet aircraft, cell phones, and computers. The purpose of using technology is to expose people to Christianity through the preaching of Christ. Independent Baptists criticize each other and call each other "modernists" without even understanding the term. The term *modernist* historically has always meant "not believing in the efficacy of the blood of Christ or the deity of Christ or the vicarious substitutionary death of Christ or His bodily resurrection or the verbal and plenary inspiration of the Bible."

One must liken the use of innovations to this illustration: If Jesus could walk on water, why did He step in a boat to teach? Why didn't He step on the water? He used what was available at that time. Why did He use a boy's lunch? Because Jesus used what was available when He needed it. Throughout all of Scripture, what was available at that time was used. Innovation has nothing to do with the theological position of modernism. Theological words are being used incorrectly to describe a resource. Modernism, by definition, has changed from a doctrinal issue to a practical issue.

It can be likened to saying, "Don't ever use a credit card; use cash. But then, don't use cash because cash doesn't mean anything." Technically, if a person is a nonmodernist, he should carry only gold coins in his pocket.

Technology, modern conveniences, transportation, and padded pews are all part of innovative growth. The church bus ministries, individual Sunday school classes by grade and gender, mid-week prayer meetings, and Bible studies, along with other transforming ideas, have helped to promote the Gospel and the cause of Christianity. At one time, air-conditioning, electric lights, pulpits, and the use of the radio were all considered innovative. Dr. Jack Hyles even used the record player to get out the *"Let's Go Soul Winning"* message. How noninnovative is the 33 rpm record player in 2008?

The inability, or perhaps unwillingness, to differentiate between compromise and innovation only adds to the confusion and criticism within our ranks. When I confronted a preacher friend of mine for critically alluding to me and to our ministry in Hammond by stating that having image-magnification screens in our auditorium is evidence of the beginning of compromise, I asked him if he felt the same way about his own ministry since he made the critical statements using a public-address system that electronically amplified his voice, similar to how the screens in our church auditorium amplify the platform. I explained that if it is compromise to amplify an image so that all can see, is it not compromise to amplify one's voice so that all can hear?

Certainly we believe in separation, and we abhor moral or doctrinal compromise. But confusing the two implies that we must return to New Testament technologies, avoiding air, train, bus, or automobile travel. It implies using horses and chariots or walking, meeting in tents or houses, using only handwritten Bibles because there were no printing presses, ridding ourselves of ballpoint pens and business suits, etc. Of course, this confusion of thought is absurd.

Utilizing innovative resources does not imply that one is following the world; rather, it is choosing the resources that best help to get out the Gospel. If television helps, then use the medium of television. Using or not using these resources is each individual church's decision, whereas preaching the salvation message is not a church's choice.

> A recent PBS special on colonial life in America in 1622 was a great reminder about how much the norms for church in our country have changed during the last 400 years. In the 1600s sermons were regularly more than two hours long, and people were fined for falling asleep in church! It was even required that everyone in town attend church weekly. Musical instruments such as the organ were considered worldly. Steeples or outdoor crosses on church buildings were looked down on as inappropriate. Playing golf on Sunday could get you put into the stocks, and having the "wrong" view about topics such as baptism could get you kicked out of the colony. Aren't you glad that at least some of those ways of doing church have changed?[25]

HYPOCRISY

Hypocrisy comes into play with the utilization of innovative technology when one condemns another for his choice of venues. Some people who strongly criticize the use of modern innovations in church make use of their own modern innovations—cell phones, text messaging, iPods, wireless hookup, websites, e-mail, etc. That person's Christianity extends only to a building he attends, rather than to him as a Fundamentally sound Christian.

"Churches are arguing more about what is appropriate and what is not, and they tend to do so based more often on their personal preference than on the teachings of Scripture. It's like reading the book of Acts, picking a favorite chapter, and throwing away the rest!"[26]

> **A common fallacy occurring in Fundamentalism is passing judgment on anyone who does not take quite the same stand on a favorite preacher or pet ideology. That person is almost always labeled a "liberal."**

MEDIOCRITY

One book that has inspired many in our Fundamental circles is *Good to Great* by Jim Collins. In this book he identifies leaders who were able to take their companies from good to great as Level 5 leaders. A Level 5 leader is characterized by a blend of humility and resolve and possesses the following characteristics:

1. He is confident enough to set up successors for success. Self-confident enough to hire competent people, he is able to hire great people to make up for his weaknesses.

2. He is humble and modest, meaning he is willing to be both introspective and self-reflective and able to engage in conscious personal development. He doesn't try to change who he is, but is able to accept the person God has made him.

3. He has an unwavering resolve.

4. He has a workmanlike diligence and is more interested in getting the job done than in putting on a good show.

5. He gives credit to others for any success and takes full responsibility for any poor results.

To become a Level 5 leader, act like a Level 5 leader. Hire the best people you can, and learn to delegate. Do not rush in to give an answer to a subordinate's problem. Be accountable for all decisions that are made. Always give credit to your subordinates for any successes, and take responsibility for any failures.

Most people find that one aspect of becoming a Level 5 leader is more difficult for them than the other. The two aspects are the humility and the will. Being willing to do whatever is needed for your cause at the expense of your own comfort involves the will. Giving credit to others for your success and accepting the responsibility for all failures requires humility.

In an interview with the *Leadership Journal,* Jim Collins expressed his surprise that his research regarding the leaders who took their companies from good to great showed many parallels to the world's great religious leaders. He made it clear that this was not something he believed to be true, but that the evidence clearly showed this parallel. Of course, the ultimate Level 5 Leader Who lived on this earth 2,000 years ago is our final example and inspiration.

When we reach a level of success that is acceptable to us or those around us, do we become satisfied? Do we stop being concerned with reaching our potential? When do we stop striving to be great and just settle for being good? What continues to motivate you when your bills are paid and your job is at a comfortable level?

Especially is this true regarding hiring practices. Remember that the "who" is more important than the "what." People should be slow to hire. Hire someone with character and someone whom you feel will be a quality employee. You can tailor their work to suit them. Don't ever hire someone whom you feel forced to hire. Hire someone whom you are confident will get on your team, be productive, and go with you to your destination. You must be confident enough to hire a strong leader and then allow him to control his area. Secular companies care enough about their company image and the safety of their employees and customers to perform background checks and drug tests and to check references from previous employers.

If a business goes to such lengths to protect its image in order to preserve its financial bottom line, shouldn't the church go to exponentially greater lengths to help preserve the integrity of the Gospel?

Ninety-five percent of nearly all church failures can trace the root cause back to an administration failure. Do not get so caught up in honing your preaching skills that you neglect your administrative skills. Read books on this topic, learn from others, and make becoming a good administrator one of your top priorities. According to a recent newspaper article, 80 percent of Catholic churches have had issues with mishandled money. Fifty percent have had a leader who failed them in the area of morality.[27]

Far too many Baptist leaders like to hide behind the guise that they do not have the problems that plague other denominations. However, too many leaders believe they are holy. Too many believe they know how to handle money. Too many assume they are excellent businessmen. Just because a man is a pastor does not mean he automatically knows everything! Among Fundamental Baptist churches, about 30 percent have dealt with a moral failure within the leadership.

Another important issue is customer service. Customer service is not a department; it is an attitude. A business with a hands-on owner usually has better quality products and better customer service. This is also true with a church. For a church to be successful, it must have a hands-on pastor. It is vital to treat all church members and visitors with respect. Telephone manners are extremely important, and it is necessary for all phone calls to be returned. We must remember that excellence is not an act, but a habit.

If God's business is so important, then why are the church bathrooms dirty, the parking lots full of potholes, the church signs dilapidated, and the light bulbs burned out? Why are the church nurseries full of broken toys and smelling like old diapers? Why is the church bulletin full of typographical errors? The first impression of a church should be that it is clean and in good repair (even if it is small). The church members should feel good about the appearance of the church. Proofreading is very important. Items such as church bulletins should not be inferiorly prepared. Care for your church's driveway, parking lot, landscaping, and signage. Make sure everything is clean and not broken. Remember that if the equipment works, the employee's morale will be better. You never get a second chance for your church to make a good first impression.

With regard to your church's finances, why should the church be run on a shoestring? Why should the finances be so poorly done and disorganized that financial reports are not released to the church members? Would you invest in stock of a company that did not publish its earnings, where the CEO was constantly out of the office, and which routinely lagged behind the curve of other companies? Because your business is a church is not an excuse to be inefficient. Any successful business must publish a quarterly earnings report and show a pattern of excellence in order to get customers to continue investing in it. A successful church must do the same in order to grow and to attract successful businessmen.

In the Bible, the word *business* is used several times. In Proverbs 22:29, the Bible says, *"Seest thou a man diligent in his business? he shall stand before kings; he shall not stand before mean men."* In order to achieve success, you must be diligent in your business. In Luke 2:49 Jesus says, *"…How is it that ye sought me? wist ye not that I must be about my Father's business?"* As pastors, you must always remember that you are an integral part of God's business here on this earth. You are God's business representative to your church and your community.

Pastor, what is preventing you from rising above mediocrity? What is keeping you from taking your ministry from good to great? Are you accepting mediocrity in order to escape the pressure created by success? The culture of success is not for everyone; it requires you to live a life of pressure. As a leader, you must learn to create a culture of success among your staff. This will require a lot of discipline and sacrifice. However, if God's business is truly the greatest business, then all the discipline and sacrifice are worth the effort.

"And in all matters of wisdom and understanding, that the king enquired of them, he found them ten times better...." (Daniel 1:20) Be ten times better!

> Many churches are in definitive patterns of decline because church members simply will not move beyond their couches of comfort. It's much easier to do things the way we've always done them rather than to get uncomfortable in the world outside the wall of the church.[28]

Dr. Towns included a chapter in his book, *The Successful Sunday School and Teachers Guidebook,* by Leon Kilbreth, "Mr. Sunday School," a layman who worked in Sunday school conferences. Mr. Kilbreth charged,

> Only 10 percent of the churches of our land today are considered effective. That means that 10 percent of the churches baptize 90 percent of the converts; 90 percent of the churches baptize only 10 percent of the converts. It's my observation that most pastors really don't want to reach people in great numbers. It takes too much out of a man; the price is too high. The constant search for new lay leadership and their training, the administering of a staff, the long detailed planning and execution of those plans, the building of new buildings, the acquiring of additional property, the moving to dual Sunday schools and worship services—all this requires a definite challenge, hard work, personal sacrifice, and pressure. So thousands of churches will remain ordinary. They will continue to remain small—and ordinary.[29]

Our Failure to Reach the Next Generation

A new study by the Barna Group (Ventura, California) shows that despite strong levels of spiritual activity during the teen years, most twentysomethings disengage from active participation in the Christian faith during their young adult years—and often beyond that. In total, six out of ten twentysomethings were involved in a church during their teen years but have failed to translate that into active spirituality during their early adulthood. Twentysomethings continue to be the most spiritually independent and resistant age group in America.

In recent years churches have begun offering their young people a style of religious instruction grounded in Bible study and teachings about the doctrines of their denomination. Their conversion has been sparked by the recognition that sugarcoated Christianity, popular in the 1980s and early 1990s, has caused growing numbers of kids to turn away not just from attending youth-fellowship activities but also from practicing their faith at all.[30]

I am a believer in the Christian-school movement. I believe it provides tremendous indoctrination for our young converts and teenagers. But I caution parents and pastors alike that the Christian school can create a false sense of security for a young adult. The substance of faith cannot be replaced by Christian nomenclature and a firm code of discipline. Christianity always has been and always will be a religion of the heart. If we capture those young tender hearts and work at keeping the heart all the way through the training process, we can raise up multiple generations of righteous stock.

Two of the major concerns many of us leaders have are how to capture those in the public schools and not lose the hearts of those in our Christian schools; for their presence is the future of our movement, and their absence spells the demise of our movement.

TWENTYSOMETHINGS STRUGGLE TO STAY ACTIVE IN CHRISTIAN FAITH[31]

20% — Churched as teen, spiritually active at age 29

61% — Churched as teen, disengaged during twenties

19% — Never churched as teen, still unconnected

Bright Spots

in the Present

"Perfection is not attainable, but if we chase perfection, we can catch excellence."
– Vince Lombardi

John 14:12, *"Verily, verily, I say unto you, He that believeth on me, the works that I do shall he do also; and greater works than these shall he do; because I go unto my Father."*

Bright Spots
in the Present

In 2005 Pastors' School honored the following "signature men." During the pastorate where each pastor is now, the average attendance has grown at least 1,000 since he became pastor of that church. These ministries certainly are worthy of being considered pattern ministries.

Missionary Rick Martin   4,377 INCREASE

Iloilo, Philippines, was calling to Rick Martin and his wife Becky to come and start a church. They began the Iloilo Baptist Church in April 1977. Twenty-eight years later the regular Sunday attendance is 4,377 people. Dr. Jack Hyles and Hyles-Anderson College awarded Rick Martin with an honorary doctorate in 1987.

Pastor Bob Gray   3,820 INCREASE

Bob Gray went to Longview, Texas, in 1980 to assume the pastorate of the Longview Baptist Temple. One hundred eighty people were in that first service when Bro. Gray became the pastor. The average attendance has flourished over the last 25 years to over 4,000 weekly.

Pastor Paul Chappell   3,585 INCREASE

Lancaster Baptist Church of Lancaster, California, called their new pastor, Paul Chappell, in 1986. At that time they were averaging 20 members. The church is currently averaging 3,605 in weekly attendance. Dr. Chappell, with the Lord and hard work, has seen an increase of 3,585.

Missionary Kevin Wynne   3,000 INCREASE

Kevin and Deborah Wynne heard the call of Mexico City in 1982. After graduating from Hyles-Anderson College with both his B.S. and M.Div., Dr. Wynne started the Iglesia Bautista Monte Sion. Starting with only his family, the last 23 years have yielded an astounding growth of 3,000. He was given an honorary doctorate in 1999 by his alma mater.

Pastor Ed Laurena   2,500 INCREASE

In 1978 Ed Laurena started the Christian Bible Baptist Church of Laguna, Philippines. Dr. Laurena started with just a handful. The Christian Bible Baptist Church now runs about 2,500 in its Sunday services. Bro. Laurena received his honorary doctorate at Pastors' School in 2002.

Pastor Gil Laurena   2,500 INCREASE

Gil Laurena went to Taguig, Metro Manila, in the Philippines to start the Christian Soldiers Impact Tabernacle in 1989, after working with his brother Ed Laurena in Laguna. In the past 16 years this thriving church has grown from nothing to 2,500 in weekly attendance. Pastor Gil Laurena was given an honorary doctorate at Pastors' School in 2002.

Pastor Keith Gomez   2,169 INCREASE

After graduating in 1982 with his B.S. degree, Keith Gomez assumed the pastorate of the Northwest Bible Baptist Church in Prospect Heights, Illinois, while it was averaging 31 in attendance. Pastor Gomez and the Northwest Bible Baptist Church later moved to Elgin, Illinois, and have seen an increase of 2,138. Ten years into his pastorate, Bro. Gomez was awarded an honorary doctorate from Hyles-Anderson College.

Pastor Doug Fisher   1,770 INCREASE

Doug and Pattie Fisher went to Lemon Grove, California, back in 1983 to take on the pastorate of the Lighthouse Baptist Church. When he became the pastor, the church was running only 30 in attendance. Today 1,800 people enjoy the Sunday services. In his 22 years as pastor, Bro. Fisher has helped his church climb to the next level.

Pastor John Morgan   1,300 INCREASE

On February 22, 1976, John Morgan started the International Baptist Church in Brooklyn, New York, with only 29 people in his first service. With his faithfulness and help from God, the church now draws a crowd of 1,300 every week. Pastor Morgan was given an honorary doctorate from Hyles-Anderson College in 1992.

Pastor Jeff Fugate   1,290 INCREASE

In May 1991 Clay Mills Road Baptist church was in need of a pastor. Jeff and Michelle Fugate moved to Lexington, Kentucky, to pastor this congregation of 60. Today the congregation has flourished to one of 1,350. Pastor Fugate has received an honorary doctorate from both Hyles-Anderson College and Oklahoma Baptist College.

Pastor Kevin Trout   1,260 INCREASE

Kevin Trout went to York, Pennsylvania, in September 1988 to assume the pastorate of the Bible Baptist Church. When he became the pastor, the church was running 40 in attendance. Pastor Trout graduated from Hyles-Anderson College in 1985 with his B.S. degree, and ten years later he received his honorary doctorate from his alma mater. During the 16 years of his pastorate, the Bible Baptist Church has grown to a weekly attendance of 1,300.

Pastor Frank Gagliano   1,216 INCREASE

Frank Gagliano assumed the pastorate of the South Haven Baptist Church in Springfield, Tennessee, in October 1986. At the time, the church was averaging approximately 140 people each week. After 19 years of diligence, Pastor Gagliano now holds services for 1,356 people each week.

Pastor Mickey Carter   1,211 INCREASE

When the Landmark Baptist Church of Haines City, Florida, was running 39 in attendance, Mickey Carter assumed the pastorate. Currently the church is averaging 1,250 in weekly attendance. In the 34 years of the ministry of Pastor Carter and his wife Sonja, the church has seen a growth of 1,211.

Missionary Luis Ramos   1,200 INCREASE

After receiving his B.S. from Hyles-Anderson College, Luis Ramos went to San Luis Potosi, Mexico, to start the Iglesia Biblica Bautista de San Luis Potosi. Through hard work, patience, and faithfulness, Bro. Ramos and God have helped the church to grow to 1,200 since its start in 1990. Pastor Ramos received an honorary doctorate from Hyles-Anderson College in 2000.

Pastor Lonnie Mattingly   1,142 INCREASE

The Shawnee Baptist Church was blessed in December 1972 when Lonnie Mattingly came to Louisville, Kentucky, to become their new pastor. At the initiation of his pastorate, the regular weekly attendance was approximately 63. Thirty-three years later an increase of 1,142 has boosted their weekly attendance to 1,205.

Pastor Eric Capaci   1,100 INCREASE

Hot Springs, Arkansas, became the home of Eric and Carolann Capaci in 1993 when they moved from Hammond, Indiana, to start the Gospel Light Baptist Church. Starting from nothing, Bro. Capaci, the Lord, and a lot of hard work increased the average Sunday school attendance to 1,100. Hyles-Anderson College is where Bro. Capaci earned his B.S. and M.Div. and received his honorary doctorate.

Pastor Bruce Goddard   1,100 INCREASE

After receiving his B.S. from Hyles-Anderson College, Bruce Goddard started Faith Baptist Church in Wildomar, California, in August 1982. Pastor Goddard and his wife Tammy began their church in a tent. As Bro. Goddard remained diligent to his service to God, the church attendance increased. During the last 23 years the church has grown by 1,100. In 1990 Pastor Goddard received an honorary doctorate from his alma mater.

Where Are We Going?

In these final comments let me say first that I would hope that whatever this book stirs within you, it would not stir you to be critical, defensive, or defeatist. The research team consists of some of the finest workers I know, but we are all prone to an occasional error. We have researched our facts and have cross-referenced our findings with as many sources as we could confidently secure. That does not mean that we might not have sincerely or inadvertently presented a fact or stated a conclusion based on a mistake of insertion or interpretation. If your research differs, I would welcome your honest and sincere input.

Secondly, this book is not written to point a finger of judgment on anyone who is sincerely trying to do what he believes God would have him do. I fully understand that those of us in the Independent Baptist movement tend to be harsh in our judgments of differing works and differing models. I would hope that we could realize that God has not called us to make everyone conform to us, but that He has other sheep that are not of our pasture. My concern is not so much that other men are espousing models and methods that I believe to be unsound Scripturally, for that has always been a part of the ministry. My concern is that my Baptist brethren are often confused and even disorientated with regards to what they believe about the model and methods that have been the Baptist model and methods for centuries.

Let me put it this way. I have some very good neighbors where I live. We get along very well. Some of them are Catholic, some are contemporary worshipers, and some are Baptist, but not like I am. My wife and I felt that our duty was to be good neighbors. We have won several of them to Christ, and we enjoy the relationship that we have with them; however, we were committed to training our children within our family to model themselves after us, and thus far have accomplished that.

In a similar vein, I want my Independent Baptist brethren to be neighborly with others who differ from us in the ministry, but I want us committed to training our members and preacher boys in the model handed down to us from Scripture and our forefathers. My fear is that too many of my brethren are asking the neighbors to rear their children and to train our preacher boys and even to teach them how to fashion their marriages and families. I think that is very unwise and quite dangerous.

Allow me to suggest some practical steps to correct some of the trends this book reveals.

1. Let's go back to the book of Acts and the epistles, and let the Word of God establish our message, our model, and our methods.

2. Let's dust off the history books that demonstrate some of the great Baptists of yesteryear and examine them as part of our heritage rather than looking almost exclusively at non-Baptists for example.

3. Let's revive a passion for soul winning in our own personal lives and in our churches. And let's be sure that our goal is not to get a certain number saved or baptized, but let's have as our goal to be thorough in our presentation and to let the Father draw them by the truth we present and by the power of our own testimonies.

4. Let's get back to the powerful dynamic of the small-unit Sunday school. This is our most powerful tool for indoctrinating and mentoring new converts. Healthy, growing churches have healthy Sunday schools.

5. Let's not abandon the bus ministry. It still works, and it is still the most cost-effective and productive tool of evangelism, when organized and staffed properly. It also is the greatest tool for reaching the poor with the Gospel, which is right at the heart of our Saviour.

6. Let's get back to prayer and the Word of God. Fellow brethren, let's not deceive ourselves as to our true walk with God.

7. Let's get wise in the matters of business. If God's business is truly the greatest business in all the world, let's run it accordingly. Let's strive for perfection, knowing we can't reach it, but also knowing that in so doing, we will achieve excellence.

8. Let's be HOLY men of God–enough of the foolishness of worldly ministers, immoral ministers, and unethical ministers!

9. Let's get a vision of what we can do to fulfill the Great Commission. Let's be honest. We are NOT getting the job done, but I believe we can!

10. Let's stop criticizing one another. Stop using the pulpit to vent about another brother who differs from you. If we have sincere questions, then let's be Scriptural and talk to the brother privately. We have aired our dirty laundry before our congregations. They don't need that; it doesn't edify them, and it discourages one another. We're better than that, gentlemen.

11. Finally, but most importantly, LET'S MAGNIFY THE LORD JESUS CHRIST!

I do have much hope for the future. From our survey of approximately 1,100 churches that have sent delegates to our Pastors' School in the last 7 years, 52 percent responded, and 17 percent of those indicated they are averaging over 1,000 in weekly attendance. Further research from others shows that from a list of 35 Independent Baptist churches running over 1,000, 23 of those churches are younger than 25 years, and 19 started with less than 50 in attendance.

Our survey also showed that of the 1,100 churches, 44.3 percent saw their greatest growth last year, and 34.4 percent started a bus ministry in the last 7 years. The bus ministry can be a powerful generator for growth.

This book was written to inform, provoke, and inspire the pastors who would sincerely read it with that intent. I wanted my fellow pastors to be challenged by facts and research and good analysis. I am not "down" on our movement, but I am not happy with how things are either. I don't particularly like what I see, but I want to let that challenge me to change what is and to hand down to my children's and grandchildren's generations greater works than what we have now.

Jesus said in John 14:12, *"Verily, verily, I say unto you, He that believeth on me, the works that I do shall he do also; and greater works than these shall he do; because I go unto my Father."*

Oh how I love that statement, *"...greater works than these shall he do...."* I am fully committed to doing those *"greater works."* I invite you to join those of us who truly believe Jesus meant what He said.

Acknowledgements

Author & Chief Editor: Jack Schaap

Project Manager: David Jorgensen

Consulting Editor: Linda Stubblefield

Book Design & Layout: Beckie Sweitzer, Kristi Wertz

Contributing Editors:

Andrew Bailey	Tim Harrell	Matt Sheehy
Jim Belisle	Eddie Lapina	Victoria Siebenhaar
James Beller	Adri Ludwick	Karey Sisson
Brian Berkowitch	Bob Marshall	Mike Sisson
Kelly Cervantes	Erma McKinney	Ted Speer
Keith Cowling	Keith McKinney	John Vaughan
Pete Cowling	Danny Mendez	Tom Vogel
Mike Fish	Jack Mitchell	Daryl Whitehouse
Rena Fish	Joe Peete	Laurie Whitehouse
Linda Flesher	Terry Pfeifer	Ray Young
Belinda Gaona	Cindy Schaap	Mike Zachary

Proofreaders:

Kinda Carpenter	Jack Mitchell
Elaine Colsten	Julie Richter
Rena Fish	Linda Stubblefield
Gail Merhalski	

Additional Researchers and Contributors:

Kyle Baer
Cindy Burr
Jack Christensen
John Cole
Elaine Colsten
Jennie Corle
Mark Crockett
Wendell Evans
Josh Garrett

Bruce Goddard
Faye Jalbert
Ron Judd
Delia Luna
James MacRae
Pat McPherson
Jerry Pitsilides
Meredith Plopper
Clayton Reed

Zana Reichen
Randy Rodgers
Debbie Schutt
Fred Singleton
Beckie Sweitzer
Michelle Tremaine
Kristi Wertz
Dan Wolfe
Dan Wruck

Project Team:

Heidi Albert
Amelia Allen
Tommy Ashworth Jr.
Yasmine Austria
Julie Aviles
Christian Balderas
Santana Barton
Rachel Belisle
Susanna Belisle
Cheridith Benton
Caleb Bingaman
Jenna Blasius
Leslie Bolduc
Laura Bostick
Priscilla Bowser
Chelsea Breed
Craig Brobeck
Becky Bryan
Alyssa Butler
Kinda Carpenter
Rochelle Chalifoux
Erik Chavez
Jackie Chavez
Joshua Chavez
Nathan Comstock
David Condict
Lakin Conger
Amanda Corley
Amanda Cortopassi
Jacob Crockett
Peter Dance
Emily Dewar
Kimberly Dickerson
Stephen Dolan
Amber Eason
Susan Elliott
Celeste Encinas
Javier Esquivel

Jessica Faulds
Elizabeth Finn
Michael Fish
Jenny Fisher
Jennifer Fleck
Tiffany Fletcher
Rochelle Folks
Heather Foust
Brittany Francis
Abby Garcia
Jacklyn Garcia
Jaime Garcia
Marina Garcia
Melody Garcia
Mirian Garcia
Joanne Genske
Robert Genske
Jessica Gieseler
Hannah Goddard
James Goodall
David Grafton
Tenisha Grant
Heather Gray
Zachary Green
Aubry Greeno
Bennett Greeno
Hillary Hall
Kassie Hardwick
Britt Harrell
Dan Harrell
Mona Harris
Heidi Harshman
Jennifer Hedderman
Amy Hertzel
Tara Hooker
Rachel Howard
Damaris Ibarra
Julia James

Megan Jepperson
Jennifer Jimenez
Julian Jimenez
Valerie Johnson
Matthew Jordan
Joy Jorgensen
Adrianne Keithley
Betsy King
Rachel Kiper
Nathaniel Kramer
Jonathan Lawser
Brian Leonhardt
Barbara Livermore
Sara Lopez
Tabitha Lopez
Tabitha Lowry
Omar Magallanes
Daniel Mahoney
Rebecca Marshall
Kristen Mason
Sharon Maxwell
Steve McGraw
Eva Mendoza
Jacqueline Menjivar
Jenna Miller
Kristy Miller
Joshua Moberly
Amanda Mohat
Janna Moore
Robert Morris
Rochelle Morris
Alyssa Munson
Savanna Murray
Joshua Nowacki
Holly Perry
JoAnn Petropoulos
Kayla Pfeiffer
Brian Pitsilides

Stacy Pyne
Justin Rarrick
Ryan Reay
David Redick
David Richter
Sara Rodgers
Maria Rodriguez
Jose Ruiz
Tess Saldana
Elizabeth See
Jean Sheaffer
Jennifer Short
Jeremy Short
David Sisson
Alison Smith
Angela Smith
Michael Sparks
Joshua Stowe
Bethany Sturrock
Phoebe Sylaidis
James Tannehill
MaKaylah Tarr
Karen Tutton
Jaclyn Venzke
Heather Voshall
Travonte Walker
Matthew Wallen
Jason Webb
Jennifer Williams
Aaron Wilson
John Wilson
Christina Wolf
David Wolfe
Aaron Wright
Aris Wright
Karen Yoder